STUDIES IN
AFRICAN LAW

STUDIES IN
AFRICAN LAW

BY

JULIUS LEWIN

University of Pennsylvania Press
Philadelphia

First published in 1947 under the title
STUDIES IN AFRICAN NATIVE LAW
jointly by
B. H. Blackwell, Ltd., Oxford
The African Bookman, Cape Town, S. A.
The University of Pennsylvania Press, Philadelphia

It is here reprinted by arrangement with the author.

Library of Congress catalog card number: 77-167925

First *Pennsylvania Paperback* edition published 1971

ISBN (paperback edition): 0-8122-1018-2
ISBN (clothbound edition): 0-8122-7647-7
Printed in the United States of America

PREFACE

THE study of Native law has been seriously neglected both in South Africa and in the British colonies in Africa. There has indeed been scarcely any organized or continuous study of it and in the last twenty years, although other branches of African studies have advanced steadily, little has been published on the subject. The reason for this neglect cannot be the lack of material on which study must be based. On the contrary, ever since 1929 when Native law was recognized and applied throughout South Africa, there has been a series of law reports awaiting the attention of students. But these reports, embodying the leading decisions of the two Native Appeal Courts, are read only by the Native commissioners whose decisions on the bench must conform to them. The reports have not attracted the attention of practising lawyers because they rarely meet problems of Native law in professional work. Nor has Native law received adequate attention from social anthropologists, who are seldom interested in the issues raised by its legal recognition.

In these circumstances one who enters this untrodden field must be in doubt whether he is writing for the few lawyers concerned with this branch of law or for laymen interested in Native administration.

This book is a collection of essays written in recent years. Some have appeared in law journals, others in journals devoted to African studies; but most of them have been inaccessible to those who wish to pursue the study of Native law. My main academic interest is the relation of law to the social sciences, and I hope that the juxtaposition of some essays written primarily for the lawyer and others written mainly for the layman may assist each to see how the subject appears to the other.

The place that Native law occupies in the legal system of South Africa is so uncertain that its problems are more complex than those which lawyers normally face. Moreover, these problems arise in every branch of Native law; not only in the law of persons with its questions of marriage, guardianship, or inheritance, but also in contract, in delict, and in the innumerable questions of court practice and procedure; and, above all, they involve the conflict of laws.

It would be hazardous for any one person to attempt to deal with all the problems in so wide a field. I have not attempted this task. We have in South Africa Native commissioners and missionaries who, after long experience in one area, have become specialists in the tribal law and custom of that locality. There are also in some parts of the country a few attorneys who, concentrating on Native litigation, have acquired a special knowledge of the practice followed by the Native Commissioners' Courts in their particular province. But so far as I know, no one has previously approached the study of Native law with such questions as the following in the forefront of his mind: What is the relation of Native law to the Common law of the country, especially on the same subject ? Can Native law be developed to keep pace with the changing conditions of Native society ? What is the future of Native law in South Africa ?

These, I submit, are the questions that must be asked by the student of sociological jurisprudence if

not by the lawyer or Native administrator in every-
day practice. The main purpose of these essays is to
suggest answers to such questions.

Wherever possible I have cited in support of my
views cases heard in the courts and I have quoted
fully a number of judgments. I have done so because
I believe that the study of Native law must be firmly
based on knowledge of what the courts are doing.
I also hope that these extracts will lead other students
to study the law reports so long neglected.

JULIUS LEWIN

University of the Witwatersrand
    Johannesburg
        May 1946

CONTENTS

1

THE SOURCES OF NATIVE LAW

THE earliest sources of our knowledge of Native law are the reports of commissions appointed to inquire into particular problems. Of these the first was the Natal Native Commission of 1852. Like the other commissions which in the following generation were appointed for a similar purpose—notably, the Commission on Basuto Laws and Customs of 1873 and the famous Cape Commission of 1883—this Commission found itself faced with administrative problems mainly arising from the conflict of European or "Colonial" law, as it was called, with Bantu tribal law.

It is this subject which occupies the bulk of the literature from the middle until the end of the nineteenth century. The judicial powers of Chiefs, Natives and the criminal law, Native marriage with dowry in contrast with Christian marriage, the wholly different laws regarding inheritance—these are the things that puzzled the administration and its advisers.

Related to these administrative aspects of Native law and to the problems of its conflict with European law is inquiry into the content of Native law. The main source of our knowledge of Native law is the writings of those who record their own knowledge of it based on direct contact or observation. In this respect our knowledge is both incomplete and defective and Native law is accordingly weakened in its struggle both for legal recognition and in its conflict with European law.

Maclean's *Compendium of Kafir Laws and Customs* (1858) represents the first attempt to undertake the task of reducing Native law to writing for the information and guidance of all concerned with the administration of justice according to

1

Native law. Maclean, who was Chief Commissioner of British Kaffraria, was considerably assisted by experienced administrators and missionaries like Dugmore, Warner, Brownlee, Ayliff, and others, whose notes and comments form the bulk of the book. When the work was submitted to the Governor, Sir George Grey, it was printed by his authority "as a generally correct exposition of Kafir jurisprudence."

The next effort in the same direction was that of the Cape Commission, appointed in 1880, whose first duty was to inquire into Native law as it was then recognized and administered in the Transkeian Territories. The Commission had the benefit of Maclean's compilation which it proceeded to "supplement with some additional details of the laws and customs now existing and acknowledged, as furnished by witnesses under examination and others who have been acute observers of Native usages, as well as by administrators and magistrates who have had a practical acquaintance with them in the course of their official duty." Appended to the Commission's Report are "summaries of Native laws and customs" drawn from Maclean, from the Proceedings of the Commission on Native Laws and Customs of the Basutos, 1873, from the Natal Code of Native Law, and from the replies to a circular on marriage, inheritance, and crime. The Report of the Commission, which was published in 1883, together with the minutes of evidence, is still unquestionably the best original source of our knowledge of Native law. Written with admirable lucidity, the Report has become a classic document, and it is a misfortune that copies are now so rare that it is not readily available for reference. It contains a digest of what was known of Native law as such at the time of its publication. Its apparent adequacy may have seemed to render further inquiries or records unnecessary because another twenty-five years were to elapse before another contribution was made.

In 1909 the Transvaal Government published a booklet by Harries on *Sepedi Law and Custom*, a publication doubly welcome inasmuch as the Cape Commission's Report was naturally confined very largely to what are now recognized as the Nguni peoples and there was virtually nothing on record about the law of the Sotho peoples.

The fourth notable contribution of this kind has helped to fill the gap indicated. The publication in 1938 of a substantial *Handbook of Tswana Law and Custom*, compiled by Professor I. Schapera, marked a new stage in the process of recording Native law. For the first time a trained anthropologist had produced such a record for the express purpose of making the information it contained available in the administration of justice according to Native law. Moreover, by taking some pains to present the material as far as possible in the categories normally adopted in legal literature, he rendered his book obviously useful to practising lawyers and practical administrators. No less significant is the fact that this *Handbook* was compiled at the instance of the Bechuanaland Protectorate Administration which had commissioned Professor Schapera to undertake the work and which had provided him with facilities that enabled him to complete it within a few years.

The recording of Native law does not, of course, mean its embodiment in a rigid code, such as prevails in Natal. The original version of the Natal Code of Native Law, promulgated in 1878, was the work of a Board of Native Administration. What inquiries were made by the Board is not clear ; no doubt it relied on existing unpublished material and on the knowledge of experienced administrators. After a few years the Code was revised and in 1891 it was passed in the form of Law 19 of that year when it became legally binding on the courts. It remained unaltered until 1932 when it was again revised. The Code embodies the substance of Native law as it is applied in Natal and there is a tendency to follow it in the Transvaal.

The need to reduce Native law to writing remains. Although accurate information on almost every aspect of Bantu life has been accumulating at a rapid rate in the last twenty years, it is a remarkable fact that even to-day the customary law of most tribes remains wholly unrecorded. The main reason seems to

3

be that the work published by anthropologists has hitherto usually taken the form of a general "monograph." Such books often include a chapter or two of legal interest on marriage customs or on tribal courts or, less frequently, on inheritance ; and monographs are, of course, indirectly useful to lawyers in depicting the background against which cases must be considered, particularly in estimating the credibility of Native witnesses. But the material presented seldom makes the distinction necessary for most legal purposes between customs that might be regarded as mere social conventions and those which are "laws," that is, features essential to the validity of a legal process. As Sir Donald Cameron has pointed out, we must avoid "the confusion of mere ceremonial practices with the essential requirements of law ; for instance, dances and drumming at a Native wedding are the invariable custom, but they are not, like the payment of dowry, essential in Native law to the validity of the marriage."[1] The Native Appeal Court has also recognized and enforced this distinction.[2]

The gaps in our knowledge of tribal law are particularly large in the field of constitutional or public law, i.e. the powers of the Chief and his relation to his council and tribe, and in inheritance, in delicts, and in the law of procedure.

What Sir Alan Pim reported of Bechuanaland in 1933 is true of many tribes in Southern Africa, namely, that a compilation of tribal customary law "has now become a matter of great importance and urgency. The old Chiefs, who had a wide knowledge of the subject (a knowledge sometimes misapplied), have gone and very few remain of their old advisers who were also experts in the subject. The new Chiefs and their new advisers have not the same knowledge of the traditions of the past, and it would be of great assistance to them and a valuable adjunct to the regulated procedure which is being introduced in the tribal courts if a record were compiled giving the opinion of

[1] Tanganyika Territory Native Administration Memoranda. No. II. Native Courts.

[2] *Sila* v. *Masuka*, 9 N.A.C. (N. and T.), 1937, p. 121.

the best Native authorities available on the principles applicable to the main questions likely to be involved in cases tried in the tribal assembly. In its absence decisions will rest on no firm basis and may vary to an extent causing substantial injustice and possibly considerable economic loss. Unless a record is compiled in the near future its preparation will become much more difficult as the older counsellors, well versed in the subject, gradually die out. Whether a common standard is possible for all the tribes or whether tribal variations would have to be allowed for, it is not possible to say at the present stage. While the co-operation of the Chiefs and of the leading members of the tribes would be essential to the carrying out of this project, it could not be left to their unassisted efforts as was, I understand, the method adopted in compiling the partial record of customs in Basutoland. The position is much more complicated in Bechuanaland with its numerous tribes, and the record could only be adequate if it was drawn up on comprehensive and scientific lines. So far as possible it should be uniform for the different tribes. The advantages from such a compilation would be great, more especially as an adjunct to the Proclamation regulating the procedure of the tribal courts. The chief danger is that its compilation might tend to crystallize a custom in which a change had become desirable. This could be guarded against by treating it as a general standard, departures from which should be explained, and not as an absolutely binding law. The gradual development of existing customs in the directions determined by the changed conditions of modern times should furnish results of great interest."[3]

The publications mentioned above constitute the main primary sources of our knowledge of Native law. During the past forty or fifty years, however, the reported decisions of courts of law administering justice according to Native law have grown to be the major secondary source.

In the Transkeian Territories since 1894 there has been a Native Appeal Court and in Natal since 1899 there has been a

[3] Cmd. 4368. Paragraph 218.

5

Native High Court whose judgments in important cases have been collected and published as precedents. Since 1929 these have been extended year by year by the new series of official Reports which embody the decisions of the two divisions of the Native Appeal Court established under the Native Administration Act and superseding the old Transkeian and Natal courts. These series of law reports[4] now form the indispensable basis for the study of Native law in practice. In addition, the Prentice-Hall Weekly Legal Service supplies prompt, if brief, reports of cases heard in the Native Appeal Courts.

Scrutiny of the reports shows that the courts regard as authoritative the primary sources mentioned above and also the text-books mentioned below. They also quite frequently refer to the work of anthropologists, whether in the form of books or of papers in journals, for guidance in regard to particular customs. But it should be remembered that as these courts are applying Native law, the judges are entitled to rely on their own knowledge of Native law. To the extent that they do so, the reports constitute a primary as well as a secondary source of knowledge. In addition, the courts are empowered to summon Native assessors to advise them on points of law that arise in the course of a case on which precedents or indeed any kind of information is lacking. The replies of the assessors, who are usually men of distinction in the tribe, are duly recorded whether or not the court accepts their view of the matter in issue.

Cases involving discussion of Native law also occasionally come before the various provincial divisions of the ordinary Supreme Court, and they are then reported in the ordinary law reports. This happened more frequently before 1929 than it does now. When such cases do arise, however, they are worth special attention because these courts, unlike the Native Appeal Courts, normally apply the Common, *i.e.* Roman-Dutch law, and are therefore not presumed to know Native law, of which they consequently hear expert evidence if necessary.

[4] A complete list is to be found in the full biography which I contributed to *Bantu Studies*, June, 1941.

If full use has not hitherto been made of all these volumes of reports in the study of Native law, one reason may well be their relative inaccessibility. It is extremely hard to find a full set of them in any one library; and missing volumes in a series of law reports, which are all closely inter-related, are the despair of the student. To make the inquirer's task harder, there has been no regular digest made of these reports (with the exception of two digests of the Natal Native High Court Reports, 1899–1915) on the lines of Bisset and Smith's Digest of South African Case Law which every year covers all the ordinary law reports. Consequently, if one wants to know whether a particular point of Native law has arisen in the past or whether a certain custom has been discussed by the courts, there is no means of finding out except looking through every volume of the reports. Both divisions of the present Native Appeal Court have now been functioning for seventeen years so that there are already thirty-four volumes of reports covering only this recent period. Some sort of regular digest is clearly desirable.

Until Native law reports were regularly published, it was hardly possible for anyone to write a text book of Native law because a text book, in the legal sense of the term, must be largely based on decided cases if it is to be accepted as authoritative.

The first text book of this kind was W. M. Seymour's *Native Law and Custom*, published in 1911, which confines itself to Native law in the Cape and which is almost entirely based on decisions of the Native Appeal Court.

The second text book, G. M. B. Whitfield's *South African Native Law*, published in 1929, was a more ambitious work if only because, as its title indicates, it took account of the possibility of developing a uniform body of Native law throughout South Africa.

Based on the law reports, it also relied on blue books, on the writings of anthropologists, and on other sources, in the attempt to cover as much of tribal law as was known and likely to be useful to lawyers or administrators. It became and still remains the best known and most frequently quoted book on the subject.

This book, like all standard legal text books, attempts to give a systematic exposition of Native law, and to the degree that the author expresses his own opinions on particular questions of law, it also adds directly to our knowledge.

The third text book, and the only other one that has to date been compiled on the same basis, is W. G. Stafford's *Native Law as practised in Natal*, published in 1935. It is limited to the interpretation that legal decisions have put on the Natal Code and to a criticism of conflicting and doubtful decisions.

These text books, and especially Whitfield's, have in turn influenced the courts in making particular decisions. Native law has to-day reached a stage in which the interaction of original records, of law reports, and of text books in its development can be traced as clearly as it can be seen in any other growing body of law.[5]

Future Study

The comparative neglect from which the study of Native law has suffered in the past, leaves a rich field for future study. There is hardly a single aspect of the subject that has received adequate attention from either lawyers or sociologists.

A word may not be amiss here about the method of approach to the problems of Native law. There are some signs that in the past two distinct and possibly divergent attitudes have marked the work produced. The first is the orthodox attitude of the practising lawyer who is concerned solely with the practical needs of his fellow-lawyers in the profession. Seymour's old book on *Native Law and Custom*, or more recently, C. H. Blaine's *Native Courts Practice* are books of this kind that were apparently written with no larger purpose in mind than helping the legal practitioner. On the other hand, the attitude to Native law of most anthropologists is such that they tend to regard it

[5] Laymen who may not be familiar with this process will find it fully described in C. K. Allen's *Law in the Making*, 3rd ed. 1939.

simply as one among many aspects of tribal culture and seldom reveal an appreciation of the thorny legal and practical problems which its recognition raises in the actual administration of justice. It is not surprising that neither of these two points of view has hitherto produced wholly satisfactory results for what is needed most of all is the recognition that law and sociology are not two unrelated studies. Happily, the connection between them has received a growing emphasis in recent years, notably in the United States of America where this relationship has formed the basis of the modern school of thought known as "sociological jurisprudence." Dean Roscoe Pound, one of its leading exponents, has summarised as follows the outlook of those who adopt this method of approach :

" They recognize the futility of a detached, self-centred, self-sufficient jurisprudence. Beginning with the proposition that the legal order is a phase of social control and, to be understood, must be taken in its setting among social phenomena, they urge study of the actual social effects of legal institutions and legal doctrines ; sociological study in preparation for law-making ; study of the means of making legal precepts effective in action ; study of the actual methods of juristic thinking, judicial decision, and legislative law-making ; a sociological legal history in which the social background and social effects of legal precepts, legal doctrines, and legal institutions in the past shall be investigated ; and, above all, study of how these effects have been brought about."[6]

There will surely be wide agreement that no more fruitful approach than this to the study of Native law could be suggested, and it is from this angle that the major problems awaiting inquiry should be tackled.

Many points of Native law are still obscure, mainly because our historical records are so incomplete and because modern field-workers do not aim at recording all the complicated detail which lawyers find in practice they require to know. This is the

[6] Article on Jurisprudence in the *Encyclopaedia of the Social Sciences*, 1932, Vol. 8, p. 484.

fact that lies behind the urgent need, mentioned above, to record the substance of tribal law wherever possible.

When that has been done, to some extent at least, it will simplify the next task, which is that of making a restatement of Native law in order to deal with the growing uncertainty about its position. The main object of such a restatement should not be to codify the law but to guide its development. Native law, like any other living body of law, is not static ; indeed, it is to-day changing rapidly, and simply to record the old tribal law may not be enough. The real purpose of recording should be to provide the basis on which bodies of tribal law may be developed towards a Native Common law that will be Union-wide in its application. Hitherto we have done very little to foster such unification as will reduce inter-tribal and inter-territorial conflicts of law.[7]

Inquiry is needed to disclose the full extent of these conflicts but there is already ample evidence that the problem they raise is a serious one. The present rules, embodied in the Native Administration Act, offer no adequate solution to the many difficulties that arise.[8]

Even larger problems of conflict than those within the field of Native law itself have emerged. The conflict of Native law with European or Roman-Dutch law is a major subject that has hardly been touched by inquiry. To what extent has Native law been recognized? Does it oust the Common law from application to Natives? Can we develop two parallel systems of law? The South African Native Affairs Commission of 1903–5 expressed the opinion that "the object of improving Native law and, as far as may be, assimilating it with the ordinary Colonial

---

[7] In his *African Survey* Lord Hailey evidently has this question in mind, when he says (p. 309) : "A comparative study of Native law as it operates to-day is clearly required and its object need not necessarily be codification. It is generally agreed that the codification in Natal, with its promulgation in 1891, has tended in the absence of periodic revisions to deprive Native law of that elasticity in adaptation which alone can enable it to meet the needs of a changing society."

[8] *See* the sixth essay in this book.

10

law should be kept in view as an ultimate goal."[9] We have done virtually nothing to cope with the issue it presented. Yet in the law relating to seduction, to women's status, to prescription, and to the incidents of marriage—to mention only a few outstanding examples—cases repeatedly occur that disclose conflict between Native law and Common law, a conflict the deeper because it is one of social ideas as well as of legal principles. The courts have not had the benefit of much assistance in their difficult task. The Conflict of Laws, often called Private International Law, is a branch of legal studies that has grown in strength and significance in the last generation. Its principles and precedents offer a guide to our own problems of conflict that we should not neglect any longer.

The Native Administration Act of 1927 marked a turning point in the history of Native law in South Africa because it made possible for the first time the Union-wide application of Native custom by the special series of courts established for Native litigants. But, like most legislation, the Act is by no means clear in its meaning on a number of vital points, and these have been interpreted in diverse ways by the courts in cases that have arisen and by administration in the course of its daily practice. What is much needed is a study of the problems in the application of Native law that have arisen *since* recognition was granted. Such a study could perhaps best be undertaken as part of a larger study of the working of the whole legal structure created by the Act. It should certainly include an analysis of the business of the Courts, *i.e.* of the types of cases that come to court.

The possibilities of inquiry in this field are numerous. Neither the Chiefs' Courts nor the Native Commissioners' Courts nor the Native Appeal Courts have yet received any close attention from independent observers, although their practice and precedents suggest a host of interesting questions. This is one of the subjects to which Lord Hailey drew particular attention in the course of his recent Survey. "There are

[9] Paragraph 233.

11

few problems," he wrote,[10] "which demand more careful study than that of an effective adjustment of existing judicial methods to meet the needs of the African Native. It is regrettable that the subject has not been brought under any comprehensive inquiry by the Governments concerned. In the Union, Commissions such as the Cape Native Laws and Customs Commission of 1883 dealt at some length with the general legal position in regard to Natives, but no specific inquiry has been made on the administration of justice."

How successfully Native law is reflecting or can reflect the changing habits and activities of the Natives is another fascinating theme that would repay investigation. The status of women, to mention only one notable instance, is known to be in condition hardly less than chaotic because the legal theories now followed do not fit the facts of the contemporary scene. It must suffice to note here that there are plenty of other problems that raise the same question.

So far we have remarked only on the problems arising in regard to civil justice because it is these that involve a knowledge of Native law. What one might call Native concepts of crime are scarcely recognized at all. The problems arising in the administration of criminal justice to Natives are therefore of a somewhat different kind, many of them falling in the field of administration rather than of law. Crime and its punishment is a subject that arouses high feeling among the Natives and yet it is one that has never been fully explored. What we need is a survey of crime and its incidence in particular areas, such as the Witwatersrand, where the number of Native offenders is known to be mounting every year. Punishment, prison administration, juvenile delinquency, and penal reform generally—all these present in practice questions that well deserve study by investigators trained in our Universities; but here it is clearly to sociologists rather than to lawyers that they will turn for co-operation in any projected inquiry.[11]

[10] An African Survey, p. 300.

[11] A commission of inquiry on these lines was appointed in 1945 and is now sitting.

2

THE FRAMEWORK OF NATIVE LAW *

A LECTURER in Native law and administration finds himself in a curious position. If he is legally inclined, he is dismayed to discover that he lacks precedent for himself, so to speak ! For in no British and in no American University is there a solitary lecturer in Native law. But if he persists, he can derive some solace from Holland where the Universities, and notably Leyden, take the study of Colonial law, as they call it, seriously. The Dutch have, indeed, set a notable example by their study of the problems of customary law in the Netherlands East Indies.

The phrase, "customary law", which I used a moment ago, is a common but not a happy one. It tends to increase the prevailing confusion whether Native law is properly the field of the lawyers or of the anthropologists. In South Africa the study of Native law has been deeply influenced by the anthropological approach. Field workers often (but not always) carry their inquiries into tribal law. Finding that primitive society does not differentiate clearly, as we do, between laws, social conventions, moral obligations and even religious ideas, and trained in a school that discourages the drawing of lines between various departments of social life, they have been content in their general monographs to give us a picture of the tribe, which may or may not include a certain amount of detail about the laws that are observed.

This task of recording tribal law is by no means complete even in South Africa where we have ampler records than any

* As this essay was originally a public address, the first person has been retained. It was previously published under the title *Native Law and its Background*.

13

other part of the continent south of the Sahara, with the possible exception of French West Africa. There the Administration has been tackling the task in good earnest. As you know, the study of primitive life is a fascinating affair, and no doubt we can easily understand why field workers have concentrated on the complexities of kinship, the vagaries of witchcraft, or the subtleties of ancestor-worship in preference to undertaking the dull work of recording the substance of primitive law in a way that would win the appreciation of puzzled lawyers and harassed administrators.

For lawyers and even legislators are capable of learning, however slowly. In time the work of the anthropologists created a mental climate that encouraged a new respect for Native customs and, above all, for Native law. And so, in the year 1927, Parliament gave a qualified recognition to Native law throughout the Union and an unqualified recognition to the central institution of Native law, the practice of *lobolo*.

That recognition obviously marks the beginning of a new period in the history of Native law. But although its significance did not escape suitable notice, I fear that it was too readily assumed at the time that the mere recognition of Native law by European law would render quite simple the solution of the legal problems that had before that date confronted the lawyers. Recognition no doubt solved some problems, but, looking back now when the new system has been working for ten years and more, one can see plainly enough that recognition also created a whole set of new and formidable problems.

Let me recall what the Union-wide recognition of Native law involved. The Native Administration Act established courts of Native Commissioners to hear all civil cases between Natives. It conferred on Native Commissioners hearing cases "involving questions of customs followed by Natives" a discretion whether they would "decide such questions according to the Native law applying to such customs", but it was also "provided that such Native law shall not be opposed to the principles of public policy or natural justice, and further

14

that it shall not be lawful for any court to declare that the custom of *lobola* or *bogadi* or other similar custom was repugnant to such principles".

Disclaiming any intention of introducing novel or untried principle, the Department of Native Affairs described the broad aim of the new legislation as "the flexible adjustment of Native law and tribal regulation together with appropriate machinery for its application".[1] In an address which he delivered at the opening of its first session, the President of the Transvaal and Natal Division of the new Native Appeal Court saw in the new courts "a system of judicature embodying simple and convenient forms of procedure, stripped as far as possible of legal niceties and technicalities, designed to meet the needs of the situation, one of the central ideas of which is to bring the legal machine within easy reach of, and accessible to, the highest as well as the lowest member of the Native community, with comparatively little expense".[2]

And in an early case heard before him the President again pointed out that by the Act "the Legislature sought to bring into being forums—Courts of Native Chief, Native Commissioner, and of Appeal—designed to suit the psychology, habits and usages of the Bantu, creating as nearly as possible the atmosphere of the *lekgotla*, to the arbitrament of which they have from time immemorial been accustomed to submit their disputes. While the attempt has been made to create forums and forms of practice and procedure approximating to Bantu conceptions of legal jurisprudence, the machine has been made sufficiently flexible to meet the needs of the Native who has emerged from the tribal state to the wider and more enlightened one of western civilization and its systems of legal jurisprudence."[3]

Up to this point all is well. No doubt we may credit anthropology with having so impressed the legislators and the administrators that they showed every intention of making the

[1] Native Affairs Department *Report* for 1922-26, U.G. 14, 1927, p. 4.
[2] 1929 Native Appeal Court *Reports*, p. 3-4.
[3] Stubbs, P., in *Motaung* v. *Dube*, 1930, N.A.C. Part I. (T. and N.) 12.

15

practical recognition of Native law take a form as close as may be to its tribal form and substance.

The purpose of the Legislature is clear. It intended to establish a triple series of courts—Chiefs' Courts, Native Commissioners' Courts, and Native Appeal Courts—in which the spirit of justice rather than the letter of the law would prevail. It hoped to reduce to a bare minimum the formalities and technicalities which laymen, not without some reason, usually associate with legal processes.

The intention was admirable ; how has it been realized ?

Well, as soon as we enter the realm of the court itself, the influence of anthropology flies out of the window while the lawyers with measured tread come in at the door. Not, it is true, the front door. That is reserved for the judge himself. But what of those side-doors, those uncertain gaps, if we may so call the Regulations to be framed under the enabling Act ?

Now every court of law must have *some* rules governing its practice and procedure. Laymen often overlook this stubborn fact, which is, however, rooted in all legal experience.

The Act accordingly gave the Administration power to make rules and regulations outlining the way in which these special courts for Natives would work in practice. The regulations were to describe the form of procedure to be observed, the manner of compelling witnesses to attend, the costs or fees that might be charged by the court and by attorneys, the method of carrying out the courts' judgments, and other incidental matters.

To carry out the provisions of the Act, therefore, rules were laid down for the hearing of cases in all the courts.

For the Chiefs' Civil Courts there are nine rules, though—ominously enough—the ninth rule is divided into five parts !

For the Native Commissioners' Courts there are forty-seven rules, some of them divided into several parts.

For the Native Appeal Court there are thirty rules and another thirty-nine when the President alone sits as a Divorce Court.

Let me for a moment compare these rules with those laid down for the conduct of civil cases between Europeans in the Magistrates' Courts. Their number is legion but they are not paraded in a formation that makes counting them a matter of simple arithmetic. I can best give some idea of their dimensions by saying that no attorney ever consults their mere text. He turns, by conditioned reflex action, to the heavy volume familiarly known as *Buckle and Jones*.[4] In that book the text of each rule is followed by the briefest of annotations referring the gentle reader to the cases which have decided what interpretation has been put upon each rule by the Supreme Court when litigants appealed to it against the decision of a magistrate who first interpreted the rules of his own court. The space occupied in the latest edition of *Buckle and Jones* by the text of the rules followed by terse annotations amounts to 244 large pages. To complete the glimpse, let me add that the table of cases cited in the book occupies another 180 pages while the index of topics mentioned runs to 55 pages.

Now the Magistrates' Courts and the Native Commissioners' Courts are alike in this respect that they are the ordinary courts in which a European or a Native respectively must normally begin an action he wishes to bring against another European or Native. And it seems that, at least on paper, the Native has a simpler, less intricate set of rules to observe than has the European before the court will hear his case and help him enforce the judgment he may obtain in his favour.

But now I come to the first of the unexpected results that the working of the system of special courts for Natives has produced in practice.

A court, we agreed, must have rules. Such, however, is the complexity of circumstances and the infinite range of possibilities latent in human transactions, that no sooner do you establish rules than you discover that the actual problems of procedure that arise in practice were not foreseen by

---

[4] Or, to be more precise, *Jones and Buckle*, (as it now is) *The Civil Practice of the Magistrates' Courts*. 4th edition, 1938.

your rules and are consequently not covered by them.

Ironically enough, the very shortness and simplicity of the rules laid down for Native Commissioners' Courts has caused many a point of practice to be taken. The question frequently arises whether the absence of a specific rule implies that the desirable rule for the court or for practitioners to follow is the same rule as that explicitly laid down for European litigation in the Magistrates' Courts.

Let me illustrate my meaning. The rules I am discussing contain no provision for the filing of a plea by the defendant, before the date when the case will be heard, in reply to the summons that he has received from the plaintiff. The result is that a plaintiff must come to court prepared to meet any defence with which he may be faced, and to prove every allegation in his summons. The issues have not been narrowed down by pleadings as they are in the Magistrates' Court. Consequently, the hearing of cases is protracted and witnesses have a wide field over which they may range in the course of their evidence. This is particularly undesirable, to put it mildly, with the Bantu whose qualities seldom include a vivid appreciation of what is strictly relevant to the proceedings and what is not. Moreover, whether the attendance at court of all the witnesses was really necessary or not, they must be paid. Frequently, too, the absence of a plea means that the plaintiff might find himself faced with a defence for which he is not prepared, and he then asks the court to postpone the hearing of the case. The court is almost bound to grant this request, although postponement increases the costs of the case to all concerned.

Hard experience of this kind had taught Native Commissioners the unmistakeable lesson that those short and simple rules are inadequate. They have, therefore, in some districts resorted to a special extra-legal arrangement with the local attorneys, whereby certain additional rules are observed.

Rules of court, whether few or many, and points of practice really require handling by lawyers. Native Commissioners certainly welcome the appearance of attorneys in a case.[5] And even if they did not, the Native love of litigation embraces also an ardent desire to have one's case fought by a lawyer. Especially when you hear that your opponent has invoked the aid of one, it is simply not done to go into court without one yourself. To-day the large majority of cases in the Native Commissioners' Courts are conducted by attorneys on both sides, and in the Native Appeal Court it is rare for a litigant to argue his own case.

The advent of attorneys and even advocates has in turn tended to increase, as it usually does, the number of points of practice and of technical issues generally that are raised. A rough calculation that I have made suggests that half the total number of cases heard in the Native Appeal Court involve points of practice, and if one includes cases depending on the interpretation of statutes, on matters of jurisdiction, on points of fact or evidence, and on questions of credibility, the proportion is even higher of cases that are concerned not with tribal custom but with issues emerging from the framework of European procedure that must necessarily surround Native law.

The Regulations framed under the enabling Act did anticipate the employment of attorneys. They lay down a comparatively low scale of costs that attorneys may charge the losing or opposite party to a suit. But the Regulations are silent as to what fees an attorney may charge his own client. Partly to protect themselves against failure to recover costs from the losing side, and partly from motives of pure gain, many attorneys now tend to charge Native clients fees that are higher

[5] Attorneys have their uses. A Native Commissioner tells me this authentic story of his experience in a country district. There were no attorneys in a complicated case before him. At the luncheon interval on the fifth day of hearing, when the plaintiff had not yet exhausted his case, the Court interpreter came to the Native Commissioner to tell him, with some hesitation, that defendant had mentioned privately that the same action had been unsuccessfully brought against him three years previously. The astonished Commissioner looked up his predecessor's records and found this to be a fact! If defendant had been to an attorney, *res judicata* would have been pleaded at the very opening of the case on the first day!

than they would charge poor Europeans and which are obviously out of all proportion to Native earnings.

Two of the chief aims of the Native Administration Act were to simplify legal proceedings for Natives and to reduce their cost. It has lamentably failed to accomplish either of these purposes.

The fact of the matter seems to be that the special courts were established and their rules framed on two main assumptions. The first was that Natives would for the most part appear in person before the court and not through attorneys and that points of practice would therefore arise but seldom. The conduct of cases was to be a homely, informal affair. The available evidence, however, all goes to suggest that experience has proved this assumption to have been invalid.

The second main assumption, there is reason to believe, was that most of the cases heard in these courts would involve questions of Native custom. But as I have already indicated, a large proportion of the litigation has come to turn on technical points of practice. When lawyers arrive on the scene, they inevitably bring with them a whole apparatus of procedure, appeals, precedents, and rules of interpretation. The interplay of these things is meat and drink to them. But it is also much more than that. In a world which cherishes above all else the twin goods of private property and of personal freedom, this apparatus, repellent as it may be to the layman, is undoubtedly the very stuff out of which the rule of law is woven. Conscious as we may all be of the obvious disadvantages of this technique of finding fact and law, we dispense with it at our peril. We must not forget what ample authority there is for the view that law itself has been "secreted in the interstices of procedure".

The inference I draw from these facts is that litigation, especially by semi-literate people emerging into the modern world, is a sufficiently complex affair to require rules for its efficient conduct. Complexity and rules inevitably bring attorneys into court and raise the cost of litigation. If we want to give the Natives an opportunity to litigate both efficiently and cheaply, we must therefore recognize that legal aid is an essential service. Yet it is one which they can ill afford. Consequently, only by organizing it as a social service can the State achieve its avowed object for the Natives.

If this were not enough to falsify the assumption that most of the cases heard would deal with Native custom, there is yet another reason—and that a very solid one—to add.

"The background of all Native law", declared the President in opening the first session of the Transvaal Native Appeal Court,[6] "is the tribal system". With respect, as the lawyers say, I venture to differ from that view. Whatever may have been the position in the past, the background of Native law to-day is not simply the tribal system but the vastly more complicated social and economic system in which the Natives now find themselves. My contention here requires little emphasis. Everyone who respects stubborn facts knows that, for good or ill, we have drawn the Natives to a varying but substantial degree into the intricate network that we call our economic system. The social process that anthropologists call "culture contact" has developed apace in the last twenty years and none but those who blind themselves to the most powerful social forces in our midst can seriously doubt that this process will continue, at least for a time as far ahead as practical men can see. Nowhere is the process more vividly reflected than in the special courts to which the Natives bring their legal disputes.

Apart from points of practice and cases of seduction, the commonest causes of action seem to arise from the sort of transactions and the form of relationships which Natives have adopted from Europeans and which reflect the underlying economic realities of their lives. Money lent, goods sold, services rendered, possession or ownership claimed of an article such as a bicycle, a musical instrument or a piece of household furniture, claims arising out of an insurance policy, and contracts of all kinds—these are the causes of action that bring Natives into court.

[6] Loc. cit. p. 7.

Naturally this applies rather more to Natives in the towns than it does to Natives in the countryside where actions arising from *lobolo* are still very common. But the business of the Native courts is to-day determined not less by the interests and activities of the town Natives than by those of the rural folk. Here again we have a fact that was not clearly foreseen when the system was established. The wider recognition of Native law introduced by the Act meant that, for the first time, Native law was extended as much to urban as to rural people.

The only possibility that the Legislature appreciated the nature of this change lies in those words that qualify the recognition of Native law in the Act. It shall be in the discretion of the Courts of Native Commissioners, says the Act, to apply Native law in cases involving questions of customs followed by Natives. The proper interpretation of this section, No. 11, is a matter of vital importance. The major difficulties arise in those cases in which the cause of action is known both to Native law and to Common (or Roman-Dutch or European) law or else to the Common law and not to Native law. Which system of law shall then be applied to the solution of the dispute?

The Native Appeal Court has recently shown a strong tendency to favour the application of Native law to the exclusion of the Common law.[7] I greatly fear that this tendency derives from the idea of "legal segregation" (the phrase is not mine but the Court's[8]), and from a desire to preserve at all costs as much of "pure" Native law as it can.

The result of this dubious tendency was clearly illustrated only the other day.[9]

A plaintiff claimed damages for the killing of his stallion by defendant's cow. Under Pondo custom damages are payable for injuries done by bulls but, according to the Native assessors, from time immemorial no damages have been paid for injuries caused by cows on the common pasture lands.

[7] *Moima* v. *Matladi*, 1937, N.A.C. (N. and T.) 40.

[8] McLoughlin, P., in *Matsheng* v. *Dhlamini*, 1937, N.A.C. (N. and T.) 89 and 91 and *Kaula* v. *Mtimkulu*, 1938, N.A.C. (N. and T.) 68 at p. 70.

[9] *Mdutywa* v. *Mvingwa*, Prentice-Hall, 6th April, 1940, R. 36.

The Court accordingly decided that the plaintiff could not succeed in his action for damages, refusing "to allow Common law to oust Native law." Its judgment is tantamount to holding that where a cause of action is known to the Common law but not to Native custom, the plaintiff must fail, and this in spite of the fact that the Act plainly gives the court a discretion whether it will apply Common law or Native law in cases involving Native custom.

Notice what this implies. If a few months later a cow belonging to the unsuccessful plaintiff in the above case were to injure a stallion belonging not to another Native but to a European, the latter could obtain damages under the Common law.

So we have this position : when a black man's stallion is injured by a black man's cow, there is no legal redress because Native custom applies ; when, however, a white man's stallion is injured by a black man's cow, there is legal redress available to the injured party because the Common law applies !

A second illustration of the same tendency occurred in the following case.[10] Plaintiff sued the defendant, his grandfather's brother, for the price of two bags of mealies, for certain herding fees, and for the refund of a sum of 16s. advanced by plaintiff for the taxi fare of a girl alleged to be defendant's daughter-in-law, made at the request of the defendant.

The plaintiff failed in his claim. The court took the view that "the creation of a debt in European fashion, as is alleged by plaintiff, is a thing unknown" ; that "it is foreign to Native custom in the circumstances to exact payment for board in this fashion" ; that "it is so unusual as to be incredible that Natives should think in terms of recompense for hospitality especially to relatives" ; and that, anyhow, good proof of specific contracts for the items was lacking.

From this one can see how hard it is for a Native to base a claim on a course of conduct that would be readily accepted from Europeans. Natives, apparently, are always presumed to act according to tribal custom. Only when clear and strong

[10] *Ngcobo* v. *Ngcobo*, 1938, N.A.C. (N. and T.) 169.

23

evidence to the contrary is forthcoming will the court apply the Common law to their case ; in all other circumstances the court is at pains to demonstrate the applicability of tribal law, whatever hardships may result.

The whole tendency I have illustrated is designed to keep Natives under Native law and only with great reluctance to allow them to share rights of action available to all Europeans under the Common law. This tendency appears to be inspired by an ideal of "pure" Native law which I believe to be an illusion. I have already indicated that there are at work social and economic forces that will in the long run frustrate it. And the broader ground of legal history confirms my view.

"The law of the ancient Babylonians, Hebrews, Romans and Saxons", Lord Hailey reminds us in the course of his magnificent *Survey*,[11] "had close analogies to what we see among the more primitive of the African peoples. If there is any peculiarity in African legal institutions, it is less one of intrinsic character than of the time at which they present themselves, for they exhibit to the modern world some of the scenes in a story which must have been enacted five thousand years ago in parts of Mesopotamia, and at later dates in Rome, Germany and Britain".

If the Anglo-Saxons had, after the Norman Conquest, been able to keep their laws free from Norman influence, they would have succeeded only in retarding the social and legal growth of their country. In point of fact, however, English law at that time came deeply and beneficially under the influence of Norman ideas and practices, especially in the realm of procedure. Although the Normans, who spoke French and wrote Latin, undertook to introduce indirect rule and to respect local custom, their advent profoundly affected the Native customs of the Anglo-Saxons. It is perhaps enough to remind you that words like "court", "judge", "jury", "debt", "pay", "contract", "heir", and "trespass", all entered the English language from legal French.

[11] p. 265.

One can point to an even more striking historical instance nearer home of culture contact as a means of legal growth.

Of the reception of Roman law in Western Europe it is hardly necessary to speak. The Roman-Dutch writers of classical authority all rely freely on Roman law and to this day the Corpus Juris itself is quoted in South African courts.

Although the British, when they took over the Cape in 1806, agreed to maintain existing judicial institutions, they found these to be inadequate, particularly to cope with the new and growing commerce. There followed the legal reforms of 1828. After that date the process of absorption was facilitated by the fact that nearly all the Judges appointed were trained in English or Scots law and could not speak Dutch. They consequently tended to turn to English rather than to Roman-Dutch sources of law and gradually substantial parts of English law were introduced into South Africa. By and large, it can scarcely be doubted that the reception of English law in the Union, more particularly in regard to commerce and to crime, has helped, not hindered, the economic and legal development of the country. In a forlorn search after the phantom ideal of "pure" law, we are in danger of turning our back on the richness of our legal tradition. What wouldn't Maine have given to study the practice of law in a country like ours whose tradition combines substantial elements of primitive law, Roman law, Roman-Dutch law, and English law !

Where the economic relations of people of different races are close and continuous, I do not believe it possible or practicable to apply one body of law to one race and another to the other race. It would have been absurd to suppose in 1828 that English law could be applied to English-speaking people in South Africa and Roman-Dutch law to Dutch-speaking people. For much the same reasons we cannot to-day simply apply Native law to Natives and Common law to Europeans.

I have so far dealt with Native law as if there were a whole body of South African Native law. In point of fact, however, what we seek to apply is tribal law, that is, the Native custom

25

followed by the tribe or group of related tribes from which the litigant comes. We must remember that there are scores of such groups whose customs vary a great deal, even within a single district of the Transvaal.

"To give but one example", says Professor G. P. Lestrade, "on the face of it not perhaps strikingly important, but on a deeper examination of very great importance in the lives of the people concerned, we may mention the variations in the distribution of the *bogadi* cattle among the family of the woman among the BaHuruthse tribes of the Marico district. There, in an area of about three hundred square miles, and at places separated from each other by no more than fifteen to twenty miles, three distinct and mutually contradictory and exclusive systems of distribution exist, each the age-hallowed and inviolable custom of the particular tribe which practises it.

"As a striking illustration of the variation of principle of great import from tribe to tribe, one might mention the rule observed by the same people, the BaHuruthse, that, once *bogadi* cattle have been handed over, they can under no circumstances whatsoever be returned; and this is in striking contrast to the practice of other Tswana tribes, to say nothing of other Sotho tribes, and of all the other Bantu-speaking tribes in the Union, where the return of *bogadi*, or *ikazi* or *thakha* or *lobolo* is not only possible, but even fairly common, for one reason or another.

"Of course, more or less unimportant details may vary, too, as might be instanced by the contrast between the Tswana as against the Xhosa method of determining the number of cattle to be handed over as bride-price. Apparently the Xhosa people deem a kind of public bargain-driving and haggling on those points as part of good manners. The Tswana people regard such an exhibition of cupidity in public as in extremely bad taste; they, too, drive the bargain, but it is done in private, with delicacy and a certain avowed distaste.

"That a whole system may vary is shown in the case of true Thonga succession to chieftainship as against the Zulu succession. Among the true Thonga, the next youngest brother of the late chief must succeed ; among the Zulu, his eldest son. This divergence led, by a devious route, to a bloody war between the two brothers, Mawewe and Muzila. And the deep chasm between the Sotho and the Zulu system of household grouping is too well known to need more than passing mention here."[12]

We have hitherto made but slight efforts to meet this situation by fostering wider uniformities and by encouraging the growth of a body of Native law common to all the Bantu in South Africa. Indeed, the mere possibility of developing a real Native Common law was misunderstood by Parliament. When amendments to the Native Administration Bill were being considered, the need for some measure of uniformity within the Transkeian Territories and also in Natal was realized, but not of a Union-wide uniformity even in matters of practice and procedure. This accounts for the curious fact that the statute provides for an appeal to the Appellate Division of the Supreme Court where a judgment of a Native Appeal Court conflicts with a previous decision given by the same court, but fails to provide a similar appeal where a decision of one Native Appeal Court is in conflict with a decision of the other.[13]

I hope that I am not leaving the impression that I am opposed to the application of Native law. I am as anxious as anyone that as much of Native law shall be applied as is compatible with the changing social and economic circumstances of the Bantu people. But, at the same time, I am equally anxious to take into account the social forces now at work which render it unlikely that the unlimited application of Native law can be made without producing grave hardship and even leading to a future breakdown of the whole legal system.

Of these social forces one of the most powerful is Christianity. Its introduction makes the legal situation in Africa quite different from what it is in India, to which we might otherwise look in order to estimate how far an indigenous

[12] Quoted by the President in 1929, N.A.C. (T. and N.) p. 6.
[13] Hansard, 16th June, 1927, col. 5148. This defect has been remedied by later legislation.

27

heritage of law can maintain itself in the face of European law. Indeed, Roman experience furnishes a closer analogy than does Indian. Bryce[14] points out that the power of assimilation of Roman with provincial law was more complete in some branches than it was in others ; and it was least complete in matters where old standing features of national character and feeling were present. In the law of property and of contract it advanced so far as to become, with a few exceptions, substantially identical. The same may be said of criminal law and the system of legal procedure. But in the law of family relations and in that of inheritance, a matter closely connected with family relations, the dissimilarities were still significant.

This phenomenon, he points out, reappeared in the history of English and Native law in India, and, we might add, in Africa. Among the causes which enabled the Romans—and may enable Europeans to do in Africa what they cannot in India, namely— to achieve one harmonious body of legal rules, was the fact that "there were no forms of faith which had so interlaced religious feelings and traditions with the legal notions and customs of the people as to give those notions and customs a tenacious grip on men's affection. Except among the Jews, Rome had no religious force to overcome such as Islam and Hinduism present in India."

In Bantu Africa not only is there no strong religion, comparable to Hinduism or Islam, supporting Native law, but its absence has left the field clear for Christianity, the spreading of which is, of course, undertaken as one of their main activities by Europeans who are deeply interested in the welfare of the Natives. It is not commonly realized either by missionaries or by lawyers that Christianity has been the chief means whereby Natives have been brought under European law. Whenever a Native marries by Christian or civil rites, he is married under the Common law. To some degree the legal consequences of his marriage are regulated by the Common law ; and to an uncertain extent he abandons his rights and duties under Native law.[15]

[14] *Studies in History and Jurisprudence*, Vol. I, p. 83.
[15] *See* the fourth essay in this book.

Accordingly, as long as Christian or civil marriage by Natives is possible and even encouraged, Common and Native law will continue to be closely interwoven in the sphere of family relations, which is still the most important branch of Native law. This close relationship—and the legal problems[16] to which it gives rise—is alone enough to dispose of the pretension that Common and Native law can be developed side by side as entirely distinct legal systems.

The creaking of the legal machinery, to which I have drawn attention, can no doubt be remedied. However we must not imagine that if we can perfect the machinery, we may rest content with our effort. Legal accidents happen even in the best regulated communities. It is inevitable under the present legal system that courts of law should from time to time give judgments that embarrass the Administration or create hardship for a whole class of people affected by the judgment.

When European courts do so, we can set in motion, sometimes very promptly, other machinery which will alter the situation. Parliament on occasion can and does amend the law with the deliberate purpose of nullifying a decision of the Supreme Court.

Now the Native Appeal Court, in the ten years since it was established, has certainly surprised both the Administration and others by some of its decisions. Yet they still stand as the law on the subject.

In the Transkei, in Natal, and in Native reserves, Native law can be amended by proclamation and has sometimes been in the past. The Transkeian *Bunga* and now the newer Ciskeian *Bunga* follow the admirable practice of appointing at every annual session a select committee on Native law and customs. When the *Bunga* itself and the magistrates endorse the recommendation of such a select committee, the Administration has

---

[16] For a remarkable decision on one of these problems, *see Mbani v. Mbani*, 1939, N.A.C. (C. and O.) 91. It is discussed in the eleventh essay in this book.

been known to act on it by issuing a proclamation embodying the desired amendment to Native law.[17]

The Transvaal still awaits its *Bunga*. Changes introduced in this way are, however, only regional changes. Fortunately, we have at hand new machinery, in the form of the Native Representative Council, which is Union-wide in its structure. I should like to see this Council also adopt the practice of discussing changes in Native law desired by the Native people themselves.

But we must not expect too much from that direction. In discussing particular amendments to Native law or to court procedure, we are in a realm where few laymen are competent to express an opinion, and where the Natives must needs trust their European friends almost blindly.

On the need for continuous revision of the law in the light of judicial decisions and of changing circumstances, it is hardly necessary to lay emphasis. Even in England, not exactly the home of law reform, the Lord Chancellor a few years ago created a permanent commission whose task it is to report to Parliament from time to time whether certain changes in the Common law are desirable.

To recognize Native law should not be to petrify it. Since the Native Appeal Court has shown itself so reluctant to encourage growth and change, we must look for another mechanism whereby the avowed aim of the Native Administration Act can be realized, namely, "the flexible adjustment" of Native law to the changing social and economic circumstances of the Native people.

Parliament, which in 1927 showed but a slender grasp of the issues involved in its legislation, might well entrust the task to a standing select committee of both Houses, and it might do this

[17] For a good example of this procedure, *see* my article on Tribal Tradition and Native Administration in South Africa, in the *Journal of the Royal African Society*, April, 1939. Both the Transkeian and the Ciskeian *amaBunga* have in recent years debated defects in the rules of the Native Commissioner's Courts. It may be noted that in the Transkei the Courts must follow virtually the same rules as the Magistrates' Courts. *See* Proclamation No. 145 of 1923.

more confidently now that its own numbers have been not only increased but enriched by the addition of seven members elected by the Natives. In the reports of such a select committee, Parliament and the Administration would have the material they now lack on which to base a policy of regular revision of Native law and custom. Law is a social institution, made and moulded by men at every stage of its development. If it fails to reflect the changing nature of other men's activities, it runs the risk of falling deeply into disrepute.

A word in conclusion. If I have seemed to stress the weaknesses of the Union's system of law for Natives, this is certainly not for any lack of appreciation of its merits. On the contrary, I believe that no aspect of its general Native policy does our country so much credit as that concerned with the application of Native law. Nowhere in British Africa has there been any effort at all comparable with ours in this field, and perhaps nowhere in the whole continent. That is why I am anxious that we should not fall below the standards we set ourselves in the beginning of our effort to secure for the Bantu people that part of their social heritage that we call Native law, while offering them full access to that part of our civilization that we call the Common law.

3

TWO FORMS OF MARRIAGE

THE Native Administration Act of 1927, as amended in 1929, draws a clear distinction between a marriage and a customary union entered into by Natives. A *marriage* is defined as meaning the union of one man with one woman according to law, but does not include any union contracted under Native law. A *customary union* is defined as meaning the association of a man and a woman in a conjugal relationship according to Native law and custom, where neither the man nor the woman is party to a subsisting marriage.

These definitions, which form the basis of the present law, make it desirable for the sake of clarity to avoid the term "Native marriage" because it is ambiguous. It may mean an ordinary marriage under the Common law, such as is contracted by Europeans and is contemplated by the first definition ; or it may mean a marriage under Native law, *i.e.* a customary union.

One of the common problems presented to the Native Comsioners' Courts is to decide when or whether certain parties actually entered into a customary union. This question scarcely ever arises for Europeans under the Common law because no marriage is valid unless the ceremony has been performed by a duly authorized marriage officer, who may be either a magistrate or a minister of religion—hence the phrase "civil or Christian rites." Certain formalities must be observed in this ceremony and certain words spoken by the marriage officer and by the parties to be married. When this has been done, the marriage is legally completed and normally there are written records to prove its occurrence should any doubt arise at a later date.

A customary union, however, is marked by no such precise legal ceremony, certainly not in point of time, nor is there normally any written record to which reference can be made later. It is this fact that creates the legal problem, as can be clearly illustrated from recent cases heard in the Native Appeal Court.

The first case[1] is authority for the view that Native law, as recognized in the Courts, does not require any particular form of ceremony in order to establish the validity of a customary union. A wedding feast, for instance, has a social but not a legal significance.

In this case M sued S and his son W for damages on the ground that W had seduced his, M's, ward, E, and for the custody of the two surviving children of the six born to E. The defence took the form of a plea that W had married E. It was common cause that *lobolo* had passed and that the woman E had been handed over to W as his wife. Finding that as there had been no ceremony, no marriage had taken place, the Native Commissioner at Carolina gave judgment in favour of the plaintiff.

The Native Appeal Court reversed this decision, holding that a marriage had taken place. The President (Mr. A. G. McLoughlin) pointed out that ethnologists have described very fully the various steps in the gradual process of Bantu marriage. Referring to no fewer than ten authoritative accounts, he summarised the concepts that emerge as follows:

"(1) The first stage affecting the attitude of the parties involves visits, pourparlers, and the exchange of social courtesies, all designed to establish concord between the groups, culminating in the consent of the *groups* to the proposed 'marriage.'

"(2) Then follows stage two when the extent of the *lobolo* is arranged and the cattle and the woman are exchanged.

"This is the important moment in so far as the legal aspect is concerned and is the contract proper of the ' marriage.' It is

[1] *Sila v. Masuku*, 1937, N.A.C. (N. and T.) 121.

frequently accompanied by other social and religious ceremonies, but as between the *groups, i.e.* the contracting parties,
this stage completes the transaction.

"(3) The third stage involves the bride *personally* and not
the groups as *contractors*. It is necessary for her to leave the
ancestral kraal formally, to which end a sacrifice is offered and
a feast is held, the ancestors being involved and the gall of the
sacrifice being sprinkled over the bride who is adorned with the
bladder symbolically. Her severance from her own group being
thus accomplished, it remains to aggregate her to her husband's
group. Here also a sacrifice serves as the medium to inform the
ancestors of her presence and again the culminating act is the
anointment of the bride with the gall of the sacrifice. Other
ceremonies are incidental.

" But these act are mere ceremonial and ritual which affect the
bride personally. They form the religious element of the proceedings, and their absence no more invalidates the completed
contract than does the absence of prayer, music, singing or a
wedding reception in a European marriage."

In the second case[2] chosen as an illustration, the illness of
the woman when she arrived at the bridegroom's kraal apparently led him to change his mind about marrying her, and the
question for the court to decide was whether he had already by
that time entered into a customary union with her. Plaintiff
claimed the return from defendant of cattle which he paid him
as dowry for his daughter. The dowry was accepted and defendant slaughtered a beast. Thereafter, by arrangement with
defendant, plaintiff "had the girl *twalaed*," *i.e.* abducted according to custom, and taken to his kraal. He saw her for the first
time two days after her arrival when he found her sick. The
next day he had her examined by a doctor who discovered that
she was suffering from tuberculosis in an advanced stage, and
that she had obviously been sick for many months. On the
following day, the plaintiff sent a messenger to report to the
girl's father, and to request that another girl be substituted.

[2] *Mbanga* v. *Sikolake*, 1939, N.A.C. (C. and O.) 31.

After several weeks' delay, during which she remained at plaintiff's kraal, the girl was fetched back to her father's kraal where she died. Her death took place about four months after the *twala*. Plaintiff sought to recover his dowry, alleging that there was no ceremony owing to the girl's illness and that no marriage was entered into.

The Native Commissioner at Umtata decided in favour of defendant, and the majority of the Appeal Court upheld this decision.

Mr. F. E. Owen, with whose judgment Mr. W. J. G. Mears concurred, said that "the essentials of a Native marriage are :—

    (i) consent of the contracting parties ;

    (ii) payment of the dowry ;

    (iii) delivery of the bride.

Anything more than this is purely optional. The second and third essentials were admittedly carried out. As to the first, it was necessary to show that plaintiff was in fact a consenting party. No express words or formula are observed among Natives to indicate the bridegroom's consent. The consent is invariably indicated by conduct. Here the action of plaintiff in paying dowry, *twalaing* the girl, and having her taken to his kraal is clearly capable of no other construction than that of tacit consent. Nothing more was required by Native law to indicate his consent, and his subsequent discovery of the girl's illness cannot alter the position."

It may be added that the court suspected that by his claim the plaintiff was really trying to circumvent Proclamation No. 189 of 1922, which abolished the custom of *ukuketa*, whereby a husband was entitled to claim the refund of the dowry paid by him if his wife died shortly after the marriage.

The President of the Court, Mr. A. G. McLoughlin, delivered a dissenting judgment in this case. He emphasized that the consent of both the bride and the bridegroom must be given, and expressed the view that the evidence showed the latter's conduct to be inconsistent with consent to the marriage. He added that the modern tendency to omit the customary practices in connection with marriage ceremonies, especially in the practice of *ukutwala*, increases the difficulties of the courts in deciding when a marriage has been completed, as in the present instance.

In the last case the court defined the three essential elements in a customary union in the Transkeian Territories. One of these is consent, and the next case[3] illustrates the confusion that may arise, when the bridegroom is away, as to whether he was married *in absentia* or whether he had merely made a proposal of marriage.

The plaintiff in the court below sued defendant and his kraal-head for certain cattle or their value in money as damages for alleged adultery committed by the first defendant with plaintiff's wife. The defence was a denial that any marriage had taken place or existed between plaintiff and the woman in question, and that there was therefore no ground for the action.

From the evidence it appeared that while he was away at work on the mines in 1935, plaintiff wrote to his maternal uncle asking him to arrange for his marriage to the woman in question. The uncle negotiated the marriage with the natural guardian of the girl, who demanded eight head of cattle as dowry. In June of that year the girl "was *twalaed* to the plaintiff's home," and five head of cattle were taken away on account by the guardian's messengers. The girl, who was given a new name, remained at plaintiff's home, put on the breast cloth, wore a handkerchief over her eyes, and performed the usual duties of a wife at the kraal.

The plaintiff returned home after Christmas, 1935, but he stayed only three weeks before returning to work on the Rand owing to pressure of debts. While at home he occupied the same hut as the girl, who remained there until September, 1936. In the following year when she was found to be living with defendant, plaintiff was advised by letter of the position and returned in November, 1937, and instituted these proceedings. It appeared that it was only after the girl had become enamoured of the defendant, who was evidently able to offer more dowry,

[3] *Neku* v. *Moni*, 1938, N.A.C. (C. and O.) 61.

that the validity of her marriage to the plaintiff was challenged.

The facts as disclosed in the evidence were placed before five Native assessors and they were unanimous in their decision that there had been a marriage in accordance with Native law and custom. The court (Mr. W. J. G. Mears, Acting President, and Mr. E. F. Godfrey) held that the essentials of a Native marriage had been complied with since dowry had been paid and accepted and the plaintiff and the woman had lived together at his kraal as man and wife.

Mr. H. F. Marsberg delivered a dissenting judgment. He said that there was no clear evidence that plaintiff returned to his home from the mines for the express purpose of consummating the union, and that he and the woman contradicted each other as to whether intercourse took place. At what point of time did the customary union take effect? The whole transaction was so in conflict with the practice of all civilized people which demands that there shall be no uncertainty in regard to the celebration of marriage, that on the grounds of public policy the court ought not to give its approval to this type of alliance. In support of his view, Mr. Marsberg cited the early case of Sofiba v. Gova (1895, 1 N.A.C. 7), where the dangers of recognizing marriages by proxy were mentioned. There the court felt that it could not uphold a marriage where the husband was not at the kraal to which the woman had been sent, and there was nothing to show that he was likely to be there within a reasonable time. The facts of the case before the court did not suggest that there was more than a proposal for marriage. Such proposals are a regular feature of Native custom and the practice is well understood.

This problem of deciding whether a customary union took place or not arises much less frequently in Natal than it does in the Transkei or the Transvaal. The reason is that the Natal Code of Native Law (Proclamation 168 of 1932, Section 59) lays down that "the essentials of a customary union are :

(a) the consent of the father or guardian of the intended wife, which consent may not be withheld unreasonably ;

37

(b) the consent of the father or kraal-head of the intended husband, should such be legally necessary ;

(c) a declaration in public by the intended wife to the official witness at the celebration of the union that the union is with her own free will and consent."

The Code also provides that when a customary union has been arranged, the kraal head or the parties concerned must report the day fixed for the celebration of the union to the chief or headman who must direct the official witness to attend at the time and place of the celebration. Within one month after the celebration of the union which he has witnessed, the official witness, the partners, and the fathers or guardians, or their representatives where necessary, must go to the Native Commissioner's office to register the union. The parties are required to sign the register after the entries have been explained to them, and they are each given, free of charge, a certificate of the union. Details of the *lobolo* paid or payable are also recorded.

Registration is accepted as conclusive proof of the existence of the union. Sometimes, however, the parties fail to register the union, but it should be noted that failure to register does not render the union invalid and registration is not essential to prove the existence of the union.[4]

But the public declaration required by the Code is an essential feature that cannot be dispensed with. In a case[5] where the bridegroom and the official witness were absent, but feasting and dancing were carried on and the bride was anointed and sprinkled with the contents of the gall bladder and "all the essentials of a Native marriage appear to have been observed except that there was no public declaration by the bride in the presence of the official witness," the court held that the union was void *ab initio*. It was pointed out that the official witness was in a position similar to that of a marriage officer in a marriage celebrated under the Common law.

[4] *Ndhlovu v. Shongwe*, 1940, Prentice-Hall Reports, R. 75.

[5] *Mdhlalose v. Kaba*, 1937, N.A.C. (N. and T.) 43.

In an earlier case[6], heard in 1922, which established the same point, the Judge remarked that the machinery for regulating customary unions had been in operation in Natal for over fifty years and "I am safe in saying that every Native resident in the Province, without exception, is well aware that no marriage can take place without the presence of an official witness to carry out his duties, and the presence of the official witness for this purpose is universally recognized by them as essential to legalize a marriage."

There is at least one qualification to be made to the view just quoted. Following a rule recognized in the Conflict of Laws, it has been held that the requirements of the Code do not apply only to unions entered into by Zulus in Natal. Where the parties were Sotho, domiciled in Zululand, and they contracted a customary union and sought redress there, they were bound by the provisions of the Code, the doctrine of *lex loci contractus* applying to the case.[7]

Divorce

Divorce presents the same problem as does a customary union, because in the Transkei and in the Transvaal the parties need not come to court in order to effect a divorce from a customary union. Where the parties separate after a quarrel, or in even less precise circumstances than a quarrel suggests, the question arises whether a divorce took place on that occasion.

The following case[8] illustrates the legal position.

M entered into a customary union with a woman thirty-three years ago, paying her father five head of cattle on account of the *lobolo* which had been agreed upon as twelve head of cattle. Thereafter the woman committed adultery with P, by whom she bore one child. She lived with P until he died, and then went to live with W, by whom she had had three children. She was still living with W at the time of the case. Her father

[6] *Mfanambana Ngubane* v. *Fana Dhlamini*, Natal Native High Court Reports, 1922, Vol. XXIV, Part II, p. 3.

[7] *Ndhlovu* v. *Molife*, 1936, N.A.C. (N. and T.) 34.

[8] *Shabangu* v. *Masilela*, 1939, N.A.C. (N. and T.) 86.

had died, leaving S his eldest son and heir. M now sued S for the three illegitimate children born to the woman (his sister) while she was living with W ; also for the woman herself, or, alternatively, for the return of the *lobolo* or its value, £20.

It appeared from the evidence that when M had moved his kraal from one farm to another, he had left his wife and her two children by him behind. "He does not say why he did not take her with him when he left. She states that he simply left her and took no further notice of her. About a year later, when he caught her committing adultery with P, he thrashed them both and was punished for assault." He never lived with the woman again nor supported her, and took no interest in his own children from the time they were infants until one of them married, when he came forward and claimed the *lobolo*.

The main point for the court to decide was whether the marriage had been dissolved when plaintiff chased away or abandoned his wife.

The court pointed out that the plaintiff's belated interest in the woman and her three children by W was probably due to the fact that the latter were growing up and would "in due time realize value in the marriage market." . . . "In these circumstances," said the President, Mr. E. N. Braadvedt, "I am of opinion that a clear case of abandonment of the woman by the plaintiff has been made out. If a husband does not support his wife and children over a period of probably twenty years or more, does not live with her during that time, looks on while a European farmer acts as their father, and takes no action against the man with whom the woman is cohabiting, such inaction must be regarded as abandonment or desertion. Unfortunately in the Transvaal customary unions can be dissolved without recourse to the courts. In Natal a divorce can only be granted by the court and a union is binding until so dissolved, however long the husband and wife may have lived apart. In the Transvaal we only have the un-written Native customs to fall back upon in deciding whether a union has been dissolved or not. There is a dearth of books of reference on Native custom. Harries, in his *Laws and Customs of the Bapedi*, states that if a husband drives his wife from his home for no just reason, he forfeits all rights to the woman, the children of the marriage, and the *lenyalo* (*lobolo*) cattle. He further says that it is not actually necessary that he should forcibly eject his wife. He may show that he no longer wants her in other ways, *e.g.* by failing to clothe her, failing to plough for her, or closing the entrance to her hut with reeds and bushes. Infidelity of a wife is not looked upon as an unpardonable offence against society or against the husband. Seymour, in his *Native Law and Custom* refers to a number of cases heard by the Appeal Court in East Griqualand, where it was held that if a wife deserts her husband and he fails to persuade her to come back, the marriage is considered as dissolved from the day on which she left him, and that his only remedy then is to enforce the return of her dowry. The courts of that Province will not permit a husband to gain by his neglect of duty, and will not let him stand aside and allow his wife to raise seed to him by other men. He further says that 'whether marriage is dissolved depends on the circumstances under which the parties are living away from each other.'

"Whitfield, in his *South African Native Law*, states that it has been held by the Transkeian Territories Native Appeal Court that the abandonment of a wife dissolves the marriage subsisting between her and her husband.

"In the case of *Somtsewu* v. *Xwazi* (3 N.A.C., Cape), Mr. W. P. Leary, Acting President, said : 'The appellant has for a number of years neglected his wife. On two occasions her adultery was reported to him and he took no action. He did not visit her, as is usually the case when wives are *telekaed*, and this indifference amounts to rejection.'

"In another case, Mr. A. H. Stanford, President of the Appeal Court, after referring to the facts, said : 'Under such condition the appellant cannot succeed. The marriage is not being annulled by the present action, but was dissolved by the appellant himself twenty-six years ago when he drove away his wife.'

"In view of these decisions, it appears to be clear law in the

Transkei and also amongst the Bapedi tribe in the Transvaal that a customary union is dissolved if a husband either drives away or abandons his wife, and that it is not essential in all cases that any *lobolo* cattle should be returned to mark the dissolution.

"To force the woman in this case to return to the plaintiff and to leave the man with whom she has cohabited for many years, or to take her and W's children from their parents and hand them over to a man who is in no way related to them, would be acts opposed to the principles of natural justice (*vide* Section 11 (1) of Act No. 38 of 1927). Whatever Native custom may be, the courts should not support it if natural justice is outraged thereby. Women and children cannot be treated as chattels."

Accordingly, the court (Mr. J. M. S. Brink dissenting) decided the case in favour of the defendant.

In Natal the grounds of divorce from a customary union are defined by the Code (Section 76) as follows :

(*a*) adultery on the part of the other partner ;

(*b*) continued refusal to render conjugal rights ;

(*c*) wilful desertion ;

(*d*) continued gross misconduct ;

(*e*) that the other partner is undergoing a term of imprisonment of not less than five years ;

(*f*) that conditions are such as to render the continued living together of the partners insupportable or dangerous.

In addition, the wife of a customary union may bring a suit for divorce from her husband by reason of (i) gross cruelty or ill-treatment on his part, or (ii) accusations of witchcraft or other serious allegations made against her by her husband. And the insanity or impotence of either party forms a ground for obtaining a declaration of nullity in respect of the union.

Divorce from a customary union is obtained only by order of the Native Commissioner's Court, and all divorces are therefore on record.

It may be added here that where Natives contract a marriage, the grounds of divorce open to them are the same as are available to Europeans. Under the Common law these are adultery and malicious desertion ; and the Divorce Laws Amendment Act, No. 32 of 1935, added two more grounds, namely, incurable insanity and the fact that a spouse has been declared an habitual criminal and has been imprisoned for at least five years after such declaration.

Reverting to the definitions of marriage and of customary union, we may now note that their purpose was not simply to clarify the distinction between a marriage under the Common law and one under Native law. A customary union is so defined as to establish its position in relation to a prior marriage by one of the parties. For Natives do not simply either marry or enter into a customary union. If they did, the legal issues would seldom be as complex as they are. Natives try to enter a customary union during the subsistence of a marriage, or to contract a marriage during the subsistence of a customary union. In the former case, the definition of a customary union renders invalid the attempt to contract one while a marriage exists. Where a man who is married purports to enter into a customary union with a woman and pays *lobolo* in respect of such a union, he cannot later under any circumttances recover the cattle. The court will take the view that the *lobolo* he paid was "incident to a union unsanctioned by law ; it was consideration given for future immoral cohabitation" because he is presumed to have known that, being married, he could not take another woman as his wife by Native custom.[9]

The converse possibility, a marriage during the subsistence of a customary union, is contemplated by the Native Administration Act (section 22). It provides that before a Native, who is a partner to a customary union, can marry another woman, he must make a declaration on oath before the Magistrate or Native Commissioner of the district in which he is domiciled.

[9] *Mkwanaza v. Twala*, 1929, N.A.C. (T. and N.) 19. This case shows the significance of the amended definition, which was actually gazetted on the day that the case was heard. See, also, the first case reported in the eleventh essay in this book.

43

The declaration must state the name of his partner or partners in the customary union, the name of every child of any such union, and the nature and amount of the movable property (if any) allotted by him to any such woman or house under Native custom.

Where a man suppressed the fact that he already had two wives by Native custom and that he intended to retain them as wives, and failed to make the required declaration, his marriage to a third woman was at her instance declared null and void *ab initio*, and the custody of the three minor children of the marriage was awarded her. "To countenance the acts of the defendant," said the court, "would be contrary to public policy as the law does not authorize the continuance or contraction of a Native union when either spouse enters or has entered into a Christian marriage for this immediately gives rise to an action for divorce on the ground of adultery."[10]

The cases that have been cited are perhaps enough to indicate some of the complications that inevitably occur in the contact and conflict of two different legal systems. Marriage by Native custom and marriage under the Common law can never be entirely unrelated, especially in their legal consequences. Their relationship often produces problems which trained lawyers find it hard to decide. No wonder that the Natives themselves rarely grasp all the possible implications in a course of conduct adopted by them.

From the legal point of view, the extension to the whole Union of the Natal system of registration of customary unions would no doubt do much to obviate the major difficulty, the problem of proof, shown in these cases, but if it is to be at all effective, it should include the registration of divorces as well ; and it would be desirable to make clear whether or not the legal validity of a union depends on its registration. But it is necessary to note that the mere registration of unions, even if made compulsory, will not by itself solve or even considerably reduce the other problems, social and moral, that are now so

[10] *Ndhlovu* v. *Ndhlovu*, 1937, N.A.C. (N. and T.) 80.

numerous in the matrimonial life of the Native because these problems are rooted in conditions that were not made, and cannot be un-made, by the law alone.

Modern Tendencies

The existence of two forms of marriage, one under the Common law and the other under Native law, and both open to the same people, produces many situations unprecedented in other legal systems. No doubt it was originally believed that Natives living under tribal conditions would retain "customary unions", *i.e.* marriages under Native law, as their form of marriage, while those who are domiciled in urban areas or who had assimilated western civilization to at least some degree would prefer to marry under the Common law.

Unfortunately, however, no such clear distinction is possible in practice. Though favoured mainly by tribal Natives living under tribal conditions, customary unions are not confined to them. Even more, marriages under the Common law, naturally encouraged by missionaries, take place among people who are living among a tribe and who are reluctant to discard all tribal traditions. Moreover, it is by no means uncommon for a man first to enter a customary union and then some years later to abandon his wife and contract a marriage with another woman. Alternatively, some men obtain a divorce from a marriage and then enter a customary union with another woman. In such cases the rights of the first and second wives and their respective children are difficult to determine.

These rights are not only those concerned with inheritance of the man's property when he dies. Among other questions that regularly arise are the rights of the woman in a customary union and her position in relation to her own or her husband's property. These questions have been settled for marriage by rules of the Common law that were laid down long ago. Lawyers know what capacity a married woman has to make contracts in her own behalf; what rights she has to acquire property by purchase or otherwise; whether she is entitled to financial support for herself and her children if she lives apart from her husband ; whether she can sue for compensation anyone who maims or kills her husband by accident; whether she has a *locus standi* in court, and so forth.

What lawyers do *not* know, however, is whether the same rules apply to a wife in a customary union as to a wife in a marriage. Sometimes, but not very often, legislation has provided the answer. We know that a man who deserts his wife and children can be compelled to support them, whether he was a party to a customary union or a marriage.[11] We also know that if he is killed in an accident while at work in a factory, his widow in a customary union can obtain compensation ;[12] but if he is run over in the street by a careless motorist, she or her guardian apparently cannot recover damages although she could do so had she been married to him under the Common law.[13] We know, too, that in certain cases a woman has, technically, a *locus standi* in court, *i.e.* she can sue or be sued in her own capacity, but in other cases she cannot.[14]

But we do not know to what extent a Native woman, whether in a customary union or even in a marriage, can own property. There is considerable confusion on the subject because the lawyers and Government officials, such as the Registrar of Deeds, in administrative practice adopt a view far more favourable to the woman than the Native Appeal Court does in legal theory.[15] Nor do we know to what extent a husband is responsible for the debts contracted by his customary wife at a trader's store.[16]

These questions are continually arising because husbands and their wives in customary unions do not stay quietly in their tribal huts, engaged in only those activities which their parents

[11] Native Administration (Amendment) Act 1943, section 4 (4).
[12] This is the practice under the Workmen's Compensation Act.
[13] *Mokwena v. Laub*, 1943, W.L.D. 43. It is doubtful if this decision was correct.
[14] Native Administration (Amendment) Act 1943, s. 5.
[15] *See*, for instance, *Matsheng v. Dhlamini*, 1937, N.A.C. (T. and N.) 89.
[16] *Zondani v. Maaske*, 18 E.D.C. 71 (1904).

and grandparents taught them, and disputing among themselves or their nearest relatives only those matters for which Native law provides a traditional rule.

To-day husbands and customary wives, either jointly or separately, enter into nearly all those transactions which are open to spouses under the Common law. They lend money to each other or to their relatives or friends. At the trader's store they buy goods of all kinds, luxuries as well as necessaries. In buying furniture or bicycles or what not, they make hire-purchase agreements. They take out insurance policies and open savings bank accounts. And after doing some or all of these things, husbands and wives (whether in customary union or marriage or both in turn) often desert each other and enter into illicit alliances that produce children legitimate neither under Native nor Common law. In due time these men and women of property die, almost invariably without leaving a will, and all with any sort of right to be considered may claim a share in the deceased's estate (which, ironically, is often larger—because of a life insurance policy—on his death than it ever was during his lifetime!).

In these complex circumstances it is no wonder that neither skilful lawyers nor experienced officials have even attempted to devise general rules of law that would settle the complicated cases that come before the courts. Family law has not been well developed even as a branch of the Common law. Its rules and precedents certainly do not cover such sets of circumstances as modern Native life now produces. Still less, of course, does Native law provide rules for the settlement of disputes or the control of conduct never dreamt of in earlier tribal life.

The result of this development can be foreseen. In its modern social and economic setting, the old tribal form of marriage, known to the law as a customary union, has acquired legal incidents and consequences that are bringing it ever closer to marriage under the Common law. As either legislation or the courts are compelled to clarify its legal implications still further, and once it is registered, as it already is in Natal, a customary union

47

will not be distinguishable in principle from a marriage. Nor will it be either necessary or desirable to maintain the present distinction. In their major legal consequences the assimilation of Native and European forms of marriage will then be complete. The only differences that remain will be *within* the Native family where legal relations may still be regulated by customs which are recognized by Native law but which do not determine the rights of persons outside the family circle.

This tendency towards assimilation will, however, affect not only the law relating to marriage and to the status of women, which is itself a crucial matter in modern Native law. The process, which was observed by Shepstone in the nineteenth century, will grow with time until it affects the bulk of Native law and custom as it is enforced by the courts. Such a development is inevitable. The path of the law cannot run in a direction contrary to that taken by the social and economic development of the country. Every year that passes brings fresh evidence of the absorption of Native society within the larger framework of European life. In these circumstances the possibility of two systems of law running concurrently in one country will disappear. It is time to recognize the fact that Native law has no future in South Africa as a system separate from the Common law of the land. It is time for that ancient term, the Common law, to acquire a new and richer significance as the law applicable alike to Europeans and Natives in the common country of white and black.

4

MARRIAGE BY NATIVE

CHRISTIANS IN BRITISH AFRICA

AMONG Britain's exports to her colonies there is an invisible one that has attracted hardly any notice, even from lawyers. It is English law. When Englishmen went abroad to found a score of colonies in the nineteenth century, they almost invariably took with them not only the Common law and equity, but also "the statutes of general application which were in force in England at the time the administration was created." At the same time, lest anyone perceive in this silent process symptoms of imperial arrogance, all the early Orders in Council, using the same phrases, enjoined lawyers and judges to apply Native law and custom "so far as it is not repugnant to natural justice and morality."[1]

Of the complications produced by this conflict of laws, few are more impressive than those arising from the marriage of native Christians in all parts of British Africa. Having been converted to Christianity, a varying but never negligible number of Africans, usually among the educated minority and often men of property, are married by Christian rites or, much less frequently, by civil rites.

It has been repeatedly assumed by the courts that the consequences of such a marriage should be regulated by English and not by Native law. The mere fact that the parties were Christians and contracted a Christian marriage under the local Marriage Ordinance is taken to be "sufficient to show that it was their intention that the marriage contract and all the consequences

---

[1] For the references, *see* my article on "The Recognition of Native Law and Custom in British Africa" in *Journal of Comparative Legislation and International Law*, February, 1938.

flowing therefrom should be regulated exclusively by English law."[2]

In point of fact, however, neither the parties nor the missionary who performs the marriage ceremony would normally be aware of its legal implications, as is shown by the problems afterwards presented to the courts.

The first question that arises is whether a native already married by Native custom has the right to contract a Christian marriage and, conversely, whether one married by Christian rites can marry by Native custom without committing bigamy. The question is no academic one; everywhere in Africa the Natives are polygamous and converts to Christianity not seldom fail to live up to the moral standards legally implied in a monogamous relation.

Legislation has partly settled the matter in most of the tropical dependencies. In Nigeria,[3] the Gold Coast,[4] Tanganyika,[5] Kenya,[6] and Uganda[7] the Marriage Ordinance provides that a person married under it (and thus by English law) shall be incapable of contracting a valid marriage under any Native law or custom. It is not clear if a marriage according to Native custom is dissolved by a subsequent Christian marriage.

In Southern Rhodesia a marriage by Native custom of a person previously married in church was held to be bigamous.[8] In Sierra Leone a marriage by Native custom is, however, not recognized as a marriage which can lead to a charge of bigamy.[9]

These provisions imply a recognition that marriage by Native custom is itself no less valid than Christian marriage. Perhaps they reflect the changing view that English law is taking of polygamous marriage as a foreign custom. It is still difficult to say

[2] *Cessario v. Goncallo,* 1 Nigerian L.R. 41, distinguishing *Cole v. Cole,* 1 Nigerian L.R. 15.
[3] Laws, Cap. 68, s. 35.
[4] Laws, Cap. 105, s. 44.
[5] Laws, Cap. 92, s. 35.
[6] Laws, Cap. 167, s. 36.
[7] Laws, Cap. 103, s. 37.
[8] *R. v. Kaodza,* [1912] S.R.6.
[9] Christian Marriage Ordinance, 1924 (Cap. 25), s. 16.

50

how far the rigid view adopted seventy years ago in the classic case of *Hyde* v. *Hyde* would be maintained to-day, for the Judicial Committee of the Privy Council has certainly recognized the validity of polygamous marriages in countries where they are lawful, and it has upheld rights based on them.[10]

In South Africa, on the contrary, the courts have in the past refused to recognize marriage by Native custom on the ground that a polygamous union is repugnant to Christian standards or civilized principles.[11]

They have withheld recognition whether the Native had in fact taken a second wife or not.[12] Incidentally, these decisions were made in dealing with the question whether the evidence of a Native woman, married in accordance with Native custom, is admissible against the man. That depends on whether she is to be regarded as his lawful wife. If she is, the evidence is not admissible ; if she is not, then it is. Yet in British colonies where Native polygamous marriages are recognized, the evidence of a woman so married has been admitted against the man.[13]

Subsequent legislation in South Africa has, however, drawn a clear distinction between marriage, *i.e.* under the Common law (which is Roman-Dutch), and "customary unions," *i.e.* marriages according to Native custom, which are now implicitly recognized.[14] During the subsistence of a customary union, a Native may contract a marriage, which apparently has the effect of dissolving the customary union ; but a Native who is married may not contract a customary union without running the risk of prosecution for bigamy.[15]

It follows from the fact that a marriage by Christian rites is a marriage under the Common law that a Native thus married

[10] *See* an article by W. E. Beckett on "The Recognition of Polygamous Marriages under English Law " in *Law Quarterly Review*, July, 1932.

[11] *Nalana* v. *Rex*, [1907] T.S. 407. Cf. *Seedat's Executors* v. *The Master* [1917] A.D. 302, especially at p. 308.

[12] R. v. *Mboko*, [1910] Transvaal S.C., 445.

[13] R. v. *Robin*, 12, Kenya L.R. (1929), 134 and R. v. *Mwakio Asani, 3* Tanganyika L.R. (1931-4), 66.

[14] Native Administration Act, 1927, as amended in 1929, s. 22.

[15] In Natal it is definitely bigamy under Law No. 46, 1887, s. 13.

can be divorced only on the grounds available under Common law or statute.[16] But the statutes are only those "of general application which were in force in England" at the date when the administration of the new colony was created. Subsequent statutes do not automatically apply to the colony. The wider grounds of divorce established by the Matrimonial Causes Act, 1937, will therefore not be available in Africa until such time as similar legislation may be passed in any colony itself.

What effect has Christian marriage on the property of the spouses? This question often arises and in several dependencies legislation has attempted to answer it.

In the Gold Coast a curious compromise prevails and one does not envy the official whose duty it is declared to be to explain to Natives who are about to marry the following provisions[17] in regard to succession in case of intestacy :—

"The personal property of such intestate, and also any real property of which he might have disposed by will, shall be distributed or descend in the following manner, viz. :

"Two-thirds in accordance with the provisions of the law of England relating to the distribution of the personal estates of intestates in force in England on the 19th November, 1884, any Native law or custom to the contrary notwithstanding : and one-third in accordance with the provisions of the Native customary law which would have obtained if such person had not been married under this Ordinance. Provided—

"(1) That where by the law of England, any portion of the estate of such intestate would become a portion of the casual hereditary revenues of the Crown, such portion shall be distributed in accordance with the provisions of the Native customary law, and shall not become a portion of the said casual hereditary revenues ;

"(2) That real property, the succession to which cannot by the Native customary law be effected by testamentary disposition shall descend in accordance with the

[16] *Ellen* v. *Jim*, [1931] S. Rhodesia L.R., 118.
[17] Marriage Ordinance (Cap. 105), 1909, as amended in 1935, s. 48.

provisions of such Native customary law, anything herein to the contrary notwithstanding.

"Before the registrar or a marriage officer issues his certificate in the case of an intended marriage, either party to which is a person subject to Native law or custom, he shall explain to both parties the effect of these provisions as to the succession of property as affected by marriage."

In Sierra Leone it is provided[18] that a Christian marriage, to which one of the parties is a Native, "shall not have any effect on the property of such Natives : Provided that nothing herein contained shall have the effect of preventing the parties to such marriage from coming to an agreement with respect to the control and enjoyment of their respective properties or of preventing such parties from disposing, by legal procedure and means, of their respective properties after their respective deaths.

"The property of parties to a marriage celebrated under this Ordinance shall, if both be Natives, be subject in all respects to the laws and customs of the tribe or tribes to which the parties respectively belong."

In Nyasaland a marriage by Christian rites does "not alter or affect the status of the parties or the consequences of any prior marriage entered into by either party according to Native law or custom or involve any other legal consequences whatever."[19]

In South Africa it is now provided[20] that, "during the subsistence of any customary union, no marriage shall in any way affect the material rights of any partner of such union, or any issue thereof, and the widow of any such marriage, and any issue thereof, shall have no greater rights in respect of the estate of the deceased spouse than she or they would have had if the said marriage had been a customary union."

But during the subsistence of a customary union, no Native can marry unless he has first declared on oath before the magistrate or native commissioner of the district in which he is

[18] Christian Marriage Ordinance, 1924, Cap. 25, s. 26.
[19] Native Marriage (Christian Rites) Ordinance (Cap. 82), 1923, s. 3.
[20] Native Administration Act, 1927, as amended in 1929, s. 22.

domiciled, the nature and amount of the movable property (if any) allotted by him to his wives and children under the customary union.

It is further provided[21] that all movable property belonging to a Native and allotted by him or accruing under Native law or custom to any woman with whom he has lived in a customary union, shall on his death devolve and be administered according to Native law and custom. All other property of whatsoever kind shall be capable of being devised by will.

In Natal it had indeed long ago been enacted that no marriage between Natives should "remove the parties from the operation of Native law, either in their persons or their property."[22]

In Southern Rhodesia it has been enacted[23] that Christian marriage "shall not affect the property of the spouse which shall be held, may be disposed of, and unless disposed of by will shall devolve according to Native law and custom."

This provision clearly contemplated that the property of a Native dying intestate should devolve according to Native custom, but that such property might be distributed otherwise in accordance with a will made by a Native. Although the right to make a will is not known to Native law, one is sometimes made by a Native who has been influenced by European ideas, especially after he has acquired rights or interests unknown to Native law or custom. Where a claim was based on such a will, it was contested on the ground that a Native could not by will vary the distribution of his property according to Native law. Another complication was the fact that the property in question was land, individual ownership of which was also unknown to Native law. The court held[24] that Native law cannot serve as a guide in determining succession to property, the ownership of which was unknown to the Native social structure. This was the decisive factor. Such ownership must be governed by the

[21] Ibid., s. 23.
[22] Law No. 46 of 1887, s. 11.
[23] Native Marriage Ordinance, No. 15, of 1917, s. 13.
[24] Komo and Leboho v. Holmes, [1935], S. Rhodesia L.R. 86.

ordinary law of the land, and Section 13 of the 1917 Ordinance (quoted above) did not apply to it.

That this decision must not be taken to mean that a consequence of Christian marriage is inevitably the full application of the Common law to the rights of the parties, was emphasised in the following year. A passage from the judgment in the case[25] sufficiently indicated the prevailing confusion. "There are exceptions of course in the application of Native law. . . . Various incidents of a civilized marriage have been applied to Natives inconsistent with Native law and custom. Such are the emancipation of a woman on marriage from the power of her guardian (*Rex* v. *Gutayi*, [1915], S.R. 49), the incidents of claiming damages for adultery (*Iden* v. *Philemon*, [1918], S.R. 140), the repudiation of the wife by the husband (*Sikwela* v. *Sikwela*, [1912], S.R. 168), and the power of the court to deal with the custody of the children (*Dayimano* v. *Kgaribaitse*, [1931], S.R. 134). But in the case of *Duma* v. *Madidi*, [1918], S.R. 59, the Native law of inheritance and guardianship was enforced, and in *Chidiku* v. *Chidano*, [1922], S.R. 55, the law of guardianship according to Native custom was also enforced. In the latter case, Tredgold, S.J., expressed the view, with which I agree, that Native customs should not be interfered with unless they inherently impress us with some abhorrence, or are obviously immoral in their incidence. The case of *Komo* v. *Holmes*, then, must be confined strictly to its subject-matter, which is the ownership and devolution of immovable property, a matter which falls outside the purview of Native law and custom."

Recent legislation[26] has attempted to clarify the position by simply depriving Natives of the benefits of "the statute law of the colony relating to the age of majority, the status of women, the effect of marriage on the property of the spouses, the guardianship of children, or the administration of deceased estates." The object of this enactment is apparently to restore Native law and custom in those spheres and to prevent the

[25] *Vela* v. *Mandinika and Magutsa*, [1936] S. Rhodesia, L.R. 171.
[26] Native Law and Courts Act, No. 33, of 1937, s. 3.

courts from exercising their discretion as in *Komo* v. *Holmes*.

The conclusions that emerge from this summary survey seem to be these. The rule that, in the absence of legislation, Christian marriage automatically involves the application of English (or Roman-Dutch) law, produces a crop of problems. Of these the worst is the case of the Native who is partly Europeanised in his habits, and to whom the inflexible application of either Native law or European law is likely to cause serious hardship. The legislation designed to deal with either the rule or its consequences varies widely from one colony to the next. Even neighbouring territories have treated the same problem quite differently and without consulting each other's experience.

A desirable rule to be followed in the difficult cases of Natives who are partly Europeanised was laid down in an old leading case[27] in Nigeria :

"The court is not bound to observe Native custom in *every* case where the custom is not repugnant to natural justice, etc., nor incompatible with any local ordinance. When the court has before it a matter which is purely 'Native,' or where all the circumstances to be taken into account are connected with Native life, habit, or custom, then, undoubtedly Native law and custom should apply. Where, on the other hand, the matter before the court contains elements foreign to Native life, habit, and custom, the court is not bound to observe Native law and custom."

In present circumstances it is obviously unwise for legislation to fetter the discretion of the court in such cases.

[27] *Cole* v. *Cole*, [1898] Nigerian L.R., Vol. 1, p. 15.

5

THE CONFLICT OF

NATIVE LAW AND COMMON LAW

LAWYERS in South Africa have hitherto paid but scant attention to Native law. Yet Native law is to-day in a stronger position and is the basis of more litigation than ever before in the history of the Union.

The Native Administration Act, No. 38 of 1927, established a series of special courts to hear civil cases between Natives—the Native Commissioners' Courts from which an appeal lies as of right to the Native Appeal Court. From the latter an appeal lies to the Appellate Division by special leave both of the Native Appeal Court and of the Appellate Division itself. (*Ex parte the Minister of Native Affairs*, 1941, A.D. 321.)

Section 11 (i) of the Native Administration Act, which lays down what law is to be applied in Native Commissioners' Courts, is as follows :

"Notwithstanding the provisions of any other law, it shall be in the discretion of the Courts of Native Commissioners in all suits or proceedings between Natives involving questions of customs followed by Natives, to decide such questions according to the Native law applying to such custom, except in so far as it shall have been repealed or modified : Provided that such Native law shall not be opposed to the principles of public policy or natural justice : Provided further that it shall not be lawful for any court to declare that the custom of *lobola* or *bogadi* or any other similar custom is repugnant to such principles."

The degree of recognition afforded Native law and custom under this section of the Act is uncertain. It depends on the construction of the section, an important question that has arisen in a number of cases. Of these the first seems to have been *Nqanoyi* v. *Njombeni*, [1930], N.A.C. (C. and O.) 18. Young, P., in giving judgment, said :

"It was argued that a Native Commissioner's Court has absolute discretion to apply either Roman-Dutch law or Native law because the working of section 11 is equally consistent with the view—

(a) that Native custom must be primarily invoked and Roman-Dutch law only resorted to when Native law does not affect the matter ; or

(b) that Roman-Dutch law should be primarily applied and Native custom only invoked in matters peculiar to Native customs falling outside the principles of Roman-Dutch law.

"It was admitted that if a true construction of Section 11 favours either (a) or (b), then to that extent the court's discretion is not absolute . . . .

"Now, in the opinion of this court, the discretion given to a Court of Native Commissioner is not an absolute discretion. We think that the true construction to be placed on this section is that set forth in (b) above, namely, that the Common law of the Union should be primarily applied and Native custom only invoked in matters peculiar to Native custom falling outside the principles of Roman-Dutch law.

"In this case the transaction (money lent) was not peculiar to Native custom, but was one common to the daily affairs of European and Native alike, and we have come to the conclusion that the Native Commissioner was correct in allowing the plea of prescription."

The foregoing rule does not, however, offer a guide to the decision in a case where the cause of action is one known to both Common and Native law, and where the application of one law would produce a different result from the application of the other.

A frequent example is the action for seduction. Where the plaintiff sued for damages for the seduction of his daughter and

58

joined the kraal-head with the inmate of his kraal as defendants, it was pointed out by the court that the action was one which could consequently only be brought under Native law, having no counterpart in that form in Roman-Dutch law. The court held that although at first sight it would appear that the judgment in *Nqanoyi* v. *Njombeni* laid down that in *every* case Roman-Dutch law should be primarily applied, in the present case Native law should have been applied. (*Magadla* v. *Hams*, [1936], N.A.C. (C. and O.) 56 at p. 58.)

The question was re-opened by McLoughlin, P., in *Moima* v. *Matladi*, [1937], N.A.C. (N. and T.) 40, where he formulated it as follows:

"(i) In some cases which come before a Native Commissioner for decision, the cause of action is known to both systems of law, Roman-Dutch and Native.

"(ii) In some cases the cause of action is known only to Roman-Dutch law or only to Native law.

"In regard to the second class of case, the Native Commissioner is required by the decision in *Mugubayo* v. *Mutato*, [1929], N.A.C. (T. and N.) 73, to apply that system of law which provides a remedy.

"In regard to the first class of case, what is the choice given the Native Commissioner? Is it a discretion whether or not to apply Native law; or is it a choice between one or other system of law, either of which affords a remedy?

"To this court it is inconceivable that the Legislature intended the choice to be the first, viz., whether to apply Native law or to reject it and to refuse to hear the case. As indicated in the foregoing comments on policy, this clearly was not the intention of the Legislature.

"The discretion then can only be in regard to the system of law to be applied.

"If, then, the Native Commissioner is given a discretion and he exercises that discretion judicially, this court is not entitled to deprive him of that discretion by directing that he must apply Common law to the exclusion of Native law. If anything, the rule announced by Holland in his *Jurisprudence* (10th ed., p. 400) that the nearer and narrower law will be applied rather than the wider and more remote, would give preference to Native law, as indeed Natal practice has established.

"For these reasons this court cannot endorse the decision of the Cape and Orange Free State Division in *Nqanoyi* v. *Njombeni* that Roman-Dutch law must primarily be applied, and it must hold that in the absence of proof that the Native Commissioner has not exercised a judicial discretion in the present case, his ruling that he will apply Native law cannot be disturbed, for the cause of action is one common to both Native law and to Roman-Dutch law."

It should be added that the issue in the case was simply an alleged loan of stock and a demand for repayment. The defendant pleaded prescription, which is unknown in Native law. The court held that it followed from the view of section 11 taken above that the contention that a defendant can fetter the Native Commissioner by plea to apply one or other system of law is untenable.

Here, then, we have the curious position that although a plaintiff can apparently decide which law he wishes to have applied to his case by citing a defendant liable under one system but not under the other (*Magadla's* case), a defendant cannot claim a similar right by pleading a defence known to one system but not to the other (*Moima's* case). Incidentally, no reference to *Magadla's* case was made in *Moima's* case.

A few months after *Moima's* case, McLoughlin, P., applied another test to the same question which arose in *Mhlongo* v. *Mhlongo*, [1937], N.A.C. (N. and T.), 124. This was a case of cash lent and advanced by plaintiff to his brother whom he now sued. Defendant pleaded prescription. The Native Commissioner, holding that the case must be decided under Common law, upheld the plea. He supported his ruling by stating that money-lending does not involve Native law and custom for money was unknown to Natives, especially as interest can be claimed on such transactions and interest is unknown to

Native law and custom. He distinguished the case of *Moima* v. *Matladi* (*supra*).

In the Native Appeal Court, McLoughlin, P., quoted van der Keessel's *Select Thesis* (Nos. VI to XXV), in dealing with conflicting systems of law in his day, viz., Roman and Dutch law:

"The rules were framed to solve the difficulty arising from conflict between two systems of law, viz., Dutch and Roman, the latter being subsidiary, but the principles involved are directly in point in dealing with the analogous position caused by parallel systems of law in this country, *i.e.* Native law and Common law. It is true that the condition of *subsidium* is not attached to one or other of these systems, and the analogy may not be complete.

"Nevertheless, it is the manifest intention of the Legislature that Native law is to have full force and should be applied in all cases where the parties clearly had it in mind when contracting with each other.

"The reasons for according Native law this recognition are set out in the cases recently heard by this court, *inter alia*, see *Mhlongo* v. *Sibeko*, [1937], N.A.C. (T. and N.), 34, *Matsheng* v. *Dhlamini*, [1937], N.A.C. (T. and N.) 89 (both of these cases dealt with the status of Native women), and *Moima* v. *Matladi* [1937], N.A.C. (T. and N.), 40.

" In order to give effect to the intention of the parties, the Native Commissioner is bound to ascertain the nature of the contract concluded by them. He cannot, as in the present case, arbitrarily rule that *ex facie* the summons a money transaction is obviously unknown to them. This reasoning is illogical since money is in itself only a token and among natives other articles served as tokens before contact was made with Europeans, *e.g.* ivory, brass rings, hoes, etc.

"It has already been indicated that the environment of the parties is not the criterion in ascertaining the law applicable (*Nxumalo* v. *Ngubane*, [1932], N.A.C. (T. and N.), 34.

"The nature of the transaction should be the test. If, for

61

instance, a *lobola* is paid in money, as is frequently done nowadays, the transaction remains a contract in Native law and enforceable as such. Obviously, too, a plea of prescription cannot hold good in such a case.

"Now the contract of loan is one which the natives have practised from time immemorial—it includes the well-known custom of *sisa*, otherwise known as *nqoma* or *mafisha*, and a loan of a beast or other equivalent for *lobola* is also well known and frequently practised. If it should happen that under this custom one man advances a sum of money to another to enable him to complete a *lobola* being paid in money, it is difficult to contend that the transaction has thereby lost its original nature, viz., a loan under Native custom.

"On the other hand, it is known that the Natives practise commerce and engage in transactions in contracts which are purely every-day common law dealings. Such undoubtedly would fall under the statutory rules of prescription.

"It is in ascertaining these distinctions that the Native Commissioner must use his discretion and use it judicially. He has failed to do so in the present instance and it becomes necessary to return the case to enable him to do so."

In *Moima* v. *Matladi* (*supra*), McLoughlin, P., followed *Muguboyo* v. *Mutato*, [1929], N.A.C. (T. and N.), 73, in the view that where a cause of action is known to one system of law but not to the other, that system which provides a remedy should be applied.

The case which established this principle was an action for damages for defamation. The Native Commissioner had upheld an exception to the plaintiff's declaration on the ground that, according to the custom of the tribe to which the parties belonged, slander was not actionable.

Stubbs, P., said that as there was no evidence on the point, the Native Appeal Court was not called upon at that stage to decide it, but "merely to decide whether, as it was open to the Native Commissioner in the exercise of his judicial discretion to hear the case at Common law, he has exercised a proper discretion in electing to decide the matter in accordance with Native law. Assuming he was satisfied that in Native law no action lay, he was not bound to deal with the matter according to Native law. Under section 11 of the Act he had power to choose whether he would try the action by Native law or Common law. If, in his view, by the former the aggrieved party would be without redress, but by the latter would have redress, then obviously he should have applied the law which provided the remedy. That being so, the Native Commissioner was wrong in taking cognisance of Native law and disregarding the Common law."

Manning, Member of Court, put the issue even more clearly. "Where a suit between Natives," he said, "is brought and based on principles known only in Native law though not opposed to public policy and natural justice, the question at issue is governed by that law. If the cause of action is one recognized by and capable of being tried under Common law, a party cannot be deprived of the ordinary civil remedy either because he is a Native or that the subject-matter is not or may not be actionable in Native law. Otherwise, all Natives, including those whose mode of life is in conformity with European ideas, would be liable to lose their rights of appeal to the courts in all civil matters* except in those involving Native custom. The fact that the Legislature has expressly recognized as actionable by Natives certain customs followed by them, does not restrict the Common law."

Goldsworthy, the third Member of Court, added : "To hold in these modern days and with Natives in their present general state of civilisation that no Native has any legal remedy for defamation in the judicial courts of the land, simply because his old Native custom would have afforded him none, would be a travesty of natural justice and a violation of the fundamental right of inviolability of person to which everybody is

* Cf. Seneloe v. Thloloe, 1935, T.P.D. 290, where it was held that the Act has not taken away the jurisdiction of the Supreme Court to try civil actions between Natives. Section 10 (7) of Act 9 of 1929 expressly preserves it in matrimonial suits.

entitled. It is interesting to note, though the court is in no way bound by such decision, that this view has been adopted by the Appeal Court in the Transkei in the case of *Mqakama* v. *Ngcongolo*, [1913], 3 N.A.C. 49, and in the matter of *Nomtitinya* v. *Mqaka*, [1912], also 3 N.A.C. 49."

The question remains which system of law to apply where cause of action is known to one but not to the other. If the rule of applying that system of law which provides a remedy is followed, no great difficulty arises. If, however, this rule is abandoned, as it has been in some later cases of delict, the result is usually to deprive the plaintiff of his remedy at Common law for the sake of recognising a Native custom that is in conflict with the Common law.

The clearest case of this kind is *Mdutywa* v. *Mvingwa*, [1940], N.A.C. (C. and O.) 34, and Prentice-Hall, [1940], R. 36. Plaintiff claimed damages for the killing of his horse by defendant's cow, the animals being both at the time on the common grazing ground of the location.

The court (McLoughlin, P.) accepted the statement made by the Native assessors in *Hlangu* v. *Mkutshwa*, [1910], 2 N.A.C. 46, that "under Pondo custom damages are paid for injuries done by bulls, but from time immemorial no damages are paid for injuries caused by cows on the common pasture lands, not even in the case of a second injury."

It was submitted in argument that it would be unjust to follow Native custom as it operates harshly and that therefore the Common law should be applied.

But the court "was not satisfied that we should push Native law aside when it suits a litigant to abandon it." The appeal was accordingly upheld and judgment given for defendant.

This decision is open to criticism on several grounds. In the first place the early case, *Hlangu* v. *Mkutshwa*, was decided in accordance with the Common law, the court remarking that Pondo custom as stated by the assessors "would seem to be very similar in its effect to the law as laid down in *Parker* v. *Reid* (21 Juta 496)." Common law and Native custom may coincide where the animal commits a sudden act of a violent nature contrary to its usual habits, but what of the assessors' statement that there is no liability "even in the case of a second injury"? Here is a conflict with the Common law, and it appears from the very brief judgment of the Native Appeal Court that it would allow Native custom to prevail in such a case. It might be added that the other cases mentioned by McLoughlin, P., refer to broad questions of policy in regard to the preservation of Native customs. Unlike the previous cases quoted above, they do not deal specifically with the construction of section 11 of the Act. Nor was any reference made to an earlier decision of the same court, *Gxarisa* v. *Magqoza*, [1936], N.A.C. (C. and O.) 36, where plaintiff succeeded in obtaining damages for injury to his horse by defendant's ox, and where the Common law was applied.

Another case of delict was *Kaula* v. *Mtimkulu*, [1938], N.A.C. (N. and T.) 68, in which the plaintiff's claim was for damages caused to his property by a fire started by defendant's minor son. McLoughlin, P., said that "the Native Commissioner had clearly erred in holding that only Common law can be applied. He must apply Native law, and in doing so he may consider whether the facts do or do not attach liability to the first defendant (the father) according to that law, and for the purpose he must hear evidence to show how the fire arose."

In the light of the foregoing decisions, it would appear that present practice can be summarised as follows:

(i) The true meaning of section 11 is that the Common law is primarily to be applied and that Native law is to be applied only where the nature of the case is peculiar to Native law.

(ii) Where the cause of action is known only to one system of law and not the other, that system should be applied which provides a remedy. This practice favours the plaintiff.

(iii) Where the action is brought in a form known to one system of law or indicating by summons or otherwise that it falls under one system rather than another, the system indicated is normally applied. The effect of this practice is to confer on the plaintiff a part, if not the whole of the discretion which the Act entrusts to the Native Commissioner.

(iv) Where the plaintiff gives no such indication, the nature of the transaction is the test; provided that when in doubt the court, following (i) above, will apply Common law.

(v) Where possible, the rules followed in the Conflict of Laws apply.

It is not suggested that these rules are satisfactory either in practice or in equity. Indeed, it is clear that the Legislature did not foresee the very difficult problems involved in the recognition of Native law. Now that the Act has been in operation for more than fifteen years, the time is evidently at hand for its revision in the light of experience.

It may be noted finally that the rule stated under (i) above is endorsed by Whitfield in his *South African Native Law*, published in 1929. He states (p. 10) that "ordinarily the courts apply the common and statutory laws of the Union, including those of the Province in which such court functions; but they may, in their discretion, apply Native law and custom under the circumstances set forth above" (*i.e.* section 11).

Stafford, however, in his *Native Law as Practised in Natal*, contends (p. 7) that, as far as Natal is concerned, the position is that Native custom shall be invoked when it provides a remedy and that the Common law can only be resorted to when no remedy lies under the former. He bases this view on the Natal Courts Act of 1898, section 80, which laid down that—

"All civil cases between Natives shall be tried according to Native laws, customs, and usages, save so far as may be otherwise specially provided by law or as may be of a nature to work some manifest injustice or be repugnant to the settled principles and policy of natural equity."

The section goes on to exclude trade transactions of a nature unknown to Native law, and provides that prescription shall not operate. Stafford points out that this section was not repealed by the Native Administration Act and must be read with section 11 of that Act.

This view is now supported by the Native Appeal Court's decision in *Kaula* v. *Mtimkulu* (*supra*). If it is correct, it means that, apart from the Natal Code of Native Law (Proclamation No. 168 of 1932), the degree of recognition accorded Native law is much greater in Natal than elsewhere in the Union.

6

THE CONFLICT OF TRIBAL LAWS

Of the formidable legal problems raised by the recognition of Native law in South Africa, few are more difficult than those arising from the conflict of tribal laws. They are due to the fact that there is to-day only a slight body of law common to all the Bantu-speaking tribes of the Union. It consists mainly of certain general rules embodied in or following from statutes passed by Parliament.* The bulk of Native law recognized and applied in the special Native courts is tribal law and custom known to and observed only by the people of a particular tribe or possibly group of related tribes.

When the transactions between people were confined to fellow-tribesmen, no conflict of laws in the sense of private international law arose. But for many years now many of the transactions of daily life have been between Natives of different tribes. A Xhosa man, for instance, might enter into a customary union with a Sotho woman. He expects to pay only a small instalment of dowry on marriage. The Sotho man, however, who is the woman's father, is accustomed to receive 20 head of cattle on the marriage of a daughter. In a dispute between them, which law should the court apply—Xhosa or Sotho? The answer may be neither because it may be affected by the law prevailing in the place where the parties to the agreement were living. They might, for instance, be living among Tembu people in the Transkei.

Conflict is one of the branches of law least touched by statute in other countries. It is therefore all the more surprising to find the Union Parliament making an attempt to solve its

* These rules are explained in my *Outline of Native Law* (*1944*).

complicated problems by enacting a single, simple rule. The Native Administration Act, No. 38 of 1927, section 11 (2), laid down that "where parties to a suit reside in areas where different Native laws are in operation, the Native law, if any, to be applied by the court shall be that prevailing in the place of residence of the defendant." This provision was identical with that in an older Transkeian law, namely, section 104 of Proclamation No. 145 of 1923, which was in turn based on section 23 of Proclamation No. 110 of 1879. This last provision made the recognition of Native law a matter for the court's discretion and added that "in case of there being any conflict of law by reason of the parties being Natives subject to different laws, the suit or proceeding shall be dealt with according to the laws applicable to the defendant." Some of the cases that have occurred since this legislation was passed illustrate the nature of the problems it was designed to deal with.

The first question that arises may be stated in this form. If both parties to a dispute are of X tribe but are living among people of Y tribe, are they deemed to follow the custom of X or of Y?

In *Tafeni* v. *Booi*, [1917], 3 N.A.C. 41, the parties were Tembus who had lived in a Basuto location for 17 years, and the marriage was arranged in a location in which Basuto custom prevailed. The court, following an earlier decision in *Patsana* v. *Daniel*, [1895], 1 N.A.C. 1, held that Basuto custom applied. The same principle was adopted in construing the statute more recently in *Mkoko* v. *Mkoko*, [1940], N.A.C. (C. and O.) 158, where it was clearly expressed as follows : "Where there is a conflict of tribal laws, the case must be decided according to the custom of the locality where the parties reside, irrespective of what tribe they belong to."

There was, however, a dissenting judgment in *Tafeni's* case, delivered by Mr. E. G. Lonsdale, who construed what is substantially the same statute in a way that produced the opposite result. "The location or neighbourhood of the parties is not material," he said, "but the case must be decided according to

69

the customs of the tribe to which the parties belong. Of course, the parties may contract themselves out of their tribal customs and follow those of the majority of their neighbours, and where this has been done or where such a state of affairs (? intention) may reasonably be inferred from the surrounding circumstances, then an attempt by one of the parties to place himself in a better position by pleading for the observance of his own particular tribal custom would not be permitted.

"The observance of their particular customs not being prohibited to Natives of a particular tribe when residing in locations mainly occupied by Natives of a different tribe, they clearly have the right to demand their recognition, and it is a matter of evidence for the court to decide the intention of the parties in regard to the custom governing the transaction.

"In the case in question both parties are Tembus. They both say Tembu law and custom was to govern the marriage arrangements, and the court must, in my opinion, decide the issue between them according to Tembu custom and not merely because the location in which they reside is mainly occupied by Basutos, according to Basuto custom."

It can, however, be taken that the Lonsdale view is incorrect. Natives are *not* deemed to follow their own tribal customs in the absence of agreement to the contrary. It is submitted that the rule is that Natives are deemed to follow the custom prevailing in the place where they live, regardless of their own tribal origin.

But that rule by no means disposes of the problem. The second type of case occurs when the parties, although both of the same tribe, each live among people of two different tribes. In *Thompson* v. *Zeka*, [1930], N.A.C. (C. and O.) 38, the parties to the suit were Tembu. The plaintiff resided in a Basuto location and the defendant in a Hlubi location in the district of Matatiele. The Basuto dowry is fixed at 20 head of cattle, the Hlubi dowry at 25 head of cattle, while according to Tembu custom no fixed dowry is agreed on.

The second defendant, who is the son of the first, entered

into a customary union with the plaintiff's daughter and seven head of cattle were paid on account of dowry. The plaintiff now claimed the balance of the dowry, namely, 13 head of cattle, alleging that at the time the union was entered into, it was agreed that Basuto custom would apply. The defendant denied this, saying that the arrangements were in conformity with Tembu custom, *i.e.* no fixed dowry was agreed on.

The Native Commissioner held that as the defendant resided in a Hlubi location, the law to be applied was Hlubi custom, relying on section 11 (2) of the Act. He accordingly entered judgment for plaintiff in terms of his prayer for 13 head of cattle, saying that instead of being prejudiced defendant had actually benefited to the extent of five head of cattle.

The Native Appeal Court, however, took a different view. "Now it is true," says the judgment, "that where the law of the plaintiff's domicile differs from that of the defendant, and when no special agreement has been made, the law to be applied is that prevailing in the area in which the defendant resides, but there is nothing to prevent the parties from entering into an agreement to pay the dowry fixed by the custom obtaining in plaintiff's place of abode, nor is there anything which would preclude the parties from agreeing that the custom of the tribe of which they are members should apply."

The court held that the Native Commissioner had erred in disregarding the evidence, but found that the plaintiff had not discharged the *onus* which rested on him of proving a special agreement to be paid dowry in accordance with Basuto custom.

The appeal was therefore allowed and the judgment of the court below altered to absolution from the instance.

Yet a third possibility was shown where plaintiff and defendant belong to different tribes but both live among people of a third tribe.

In *Matimisi v. Sawuka*, [1939], N.A.C. (C. and O.) 101, plaintiff claimed two head of cattle, being the balance of three head alleged to be due owing to the seduction of his daughter by the first defendant. The plaintiff was a Tembu, the defendants

71

Gaikas. The Native Commissioner applied Xhosa custom on the ground that "the question of what tribe plaintiff belongs to has never been raised before in this court and in Port Elizabeth district ordinary Xhosa custom has prevailed."

The Native Appeal Court said that "there is no warrant whatever for holding that Xhosa custom must prevail at Port Elizabeth. That area was never under Xhosa control nor is it inhabited exclusively by Xhosa. It is a purely European area in which numbers of Native peoples of various tribes have established themselves as servants or tenants or as residents in the urban area. The rule, if any, is that mentioned in section 11 of the Act."

In the event the court apparently decided the matter on the complicated facts of the case which it is not necessary to recapitulate here.

But the President (Mr. A. G. McLoughlin) added the following interesting "rider":

"Section 11 is ambiguous as it is not clear whether the Legislature had in mind the instance where the parties lived in the same area but came from different tribal areas with different laws, or the instance where they are in different areas each with a different system of law or custom.

"E.g. A lives in Bulwer, Natal, were *lobolo* is limited to 10 head; B in the Basuto territory in Mount Fletcher, say, where the *lobolo* is 20 head; C in Bizana where *lobolo* is not paid.

"B marries A's daughter while she resides at C's kraal.

"A brings an action against B for balance of dowry, say, at another centre, Bizana, Matatiele, Bulwer, or Cape Town, where the parties then reside.

"This is but one instance. Take another:

"B seduces C's daughter at A's kraal. The daughter has thrice previously been rendered pregnant.

"It is apparent that the principle, if any, to be deduced from the literal reading of the section must be applied with the utmost circumspection."

In addition to the examples given by Mr. McLoughlin, there

are plenty of other permutations and combinations that can be imagined. Without them, however, we already have these cases :

1. Where plaintiff is of X tribe and defendant is of X tribe and both live among Y people, they are deemed to follow Y custom.

2. Where plaintiff is of X tribe living among Y tribe and defendant is of X tribe living among Z people, the custom of Z will be applied, following the statute and in the absence of agreement to the contrary.

3. Where plaintiff is of X tribe and defendant is of Y tribe and both live where Z custom prevails, Z custom should be applied.

We have here used the word "live", which, however, begs another legal question. In legal language men never "live" in a place ; they are either domiciled there or reside in it. "Domicile" is a person's permanent home or the place where he resides with the intention of remaining there for an indefinite time. Residence would be merely temporary, however long-continued, if the person concerned does not regard the place as his home. The question has arisen whether the words "place of residence of the defendant," as used in section 11 (2) of the Native Administration Act, mean domicile or not. Fortunately, this question has been before the Appellate Division of the Supreme Court.

In *Ex parte the Minister of Native Affairs*, [1941] A.D. 53, Centlivres, J.A., said that "section 11 (2) presents some difficulties. It provides that 'where parties to a suit reside in areas where different Native laws are in operation, the Native law, if any, to be applied by the court shall be that prevailing in the place of residence of the defendant.' It was contended that the word 'residence' in this sub-section must mean the kraal to which the defendant belongs or, in other words, the place where he is domiciled, as any other interpretation would be unreasonable and inequitable. But even if the interpretation suggested were adopted, there may be inequitable results. For instance, two Natives may enter into a contract at the kraal of the plaintiff and to be performed there : in such a case, apart from section 11 (2), one would be inclined to say that it would be more reasonable and equitable to hold that the law of the plaintiff's kraal should prevail ; and even if the contract was not entered into at the plaintiff's kraal but was to be performed there, one would, unless a contrary intention were found, be inclined to apply the *lex loci solutionis*. Similar difficulties may arise with delicts. However, it is not necessary for the purpose of this case to construe the word 'residence' in section 11 (2), nor is it necessary to say that the ordinary meaning of that word should not be applied."

The judgment of the Appellate Division encourages the view indicated at the outset of this essay that a single rule like that embodied in the statute will not solve, and may even complicate, the problems arising from the conflict of laws. Centlivres, J.A., was obviously contemplating the application to inter-tribal cases among Natives of the rules familiar to lawyers in the Conflict of Laws.

There can be little doubt that this is what must be done even although considerable difficulties may be encountered in the task. For one thing, the Conflict of Laws is largely based on the doctrine of domicile. How far can this doctrine be applied to migrant Natives who form a growing proportion of litigants? Secondly, the whole problem is affected by questions of jurisdiction such as that which brought to the Appellate Division the case referred to.

In the past section 10 (3) of the Native Administration Act simply provided that "when the parties to any proceedings do not both reside in the same area of jurisdiction of any court, the court (if any) within whose area of jurisdiction the defendant resides, shall have jurisdiction in such proceedings."

Both section 11 (2) and section 10 (3) were found in legal practice to be very unsatisfactory. They have now both been amended by the Native Administration (Amendment) Act, No. 21 of 1943. Section 11 (2) now reads as follows :

"In any suit or proceedings between Natives who do not

74

belong to the same tribe, the court shall not, in the absence of any agreement between them with regard to the particular system of Native law to be applied to such suit or proceedings, apply any system of Native law other than that which is in operation at the place where the defendant resides or carries on business or is employed, or if two or more different systems are in operation at that place, not being within a Native area, the court shall not apply any such system unless it is the law of the tribe (if any) to which the defendant belongs."

Section 10 (3) was also amended so as to enlarge the jurisdiction of the Native Commissioners' Courts to hear cases not only when the defendant resides in its area but also when he carries on business or is employed there or if the cause of action arose there. These courts will now be in virtually the same position in this respect as magistrates' courts are in relation to European litigants.

Whether these amendments will enable the law in future to operate to better advantage remains to be seen. One may perhaps be permitted to doubt whether even in its amended form a rule will suffice which was originally put on the Transkeian statute book seventeen years before Dicey published the first English text-book on Conflict!

Another practical difficulty is that the statutory rule seems to have disguised from Native Commissioners and even from the Native Appeal Courts the fact that they are really dealing with problems of conflict in something like their traditional legal form. Moreover, few of these judicial officers, or of the attorneys who argue most of the cases before them, have had the advantage of studying the Conflict of Laws as part of their legal training.

Finally, it must be emphasized that when Native law was recognized it was not—and it is not now—a body of law common to all Natives. It is a whole series of bodies of tribal custom. Up to a point one can regard these tribal customs as a kind of personal law which accompanies the individual beyond the limits of his own tribe. But this view soon comes up against

75

the territorial nature of modern law, the statutory rules that have to be applied to Native law, the conflict of Native law and Common law, and the thorny problems of jurisdiction. All these factors now maintain a framework within which Native law and litigation struggle to operate. It is a framework that has already gone far to deprive Native law of the simplicity and flexibility which were its chief charm under tribal conditions, but it is one which has hitherto proved inseparable from the administration of law under modern social and economic conditions.

7

CRIME

IN RELATION TO NATIVE POLICY *

EVERYONE has his own views on crime. While law itself remains a remote and somewhat obscure study penetrated only by professional practitioners and a few academic critics, every nervous householder in South Africa discusses, if he does not dogmatize on, the subject of that branch of modern jurisprudence concerned with the criminal law and its enforcement. If he has suffered any personal loss through crime, that, of course, enhances his authority to speak on the subject.

The first result of this situation is that discussion of crime is usually divorced from an understanding of law in general and of the place of law in human life.

This is noticeably so in the field of Native administration. How often has one heard the plaintive cry, "There ought to be a law . . ."

In response to many such cries our legislature has been making laws as plentifully as any in the world; and while it rests from June to December, the public servants take up the white man's burden and, with regulations and proclamations more numerous and prolix than the statutes and ordinances, it carries on the making of laws, not least of those specially affecting Natives.

So the State is amply armed with laws, including the vast array of legislation that makes it a criminal offence for an African to do this or that or to refrain from doing this or that.

Yet crime and the activities of law-breakers show no sign of diminishing, nor is "the Native problem" any nearer a

* An address delivered to the Penal Reform Conference in Johannesburg on 25 June, 1945.

"solution". Indeed, if we are to believe our newspapers, every now and then, especially when other news is lacking, whole waves of crime assail our cities, and the Native problem grows bigger with every session of Parliament!

This in turn leads to a clamour that the laws should be enforced against the law-breakers. The public will presumably not be satisfied until it can read in the same newspapers that at least some of the law-breakers have been safely put in prison. Then everyone feels a bit better. But the situation itself is in fact no better; it may even be worse.

It may be worse because this chain of events—crime, clamour, commitment—is a continuous one that has been proceeding now for two or more generations in growing volume. We have now reached a point of time where there is a steady stream of men emerging from prison only to be committed to prison again after having broken more laws if not more heads as well.

The failure of law to prevent crime can be traced to certain major considerations. First is the current confusion which labels as crime not only serious offences committed by persistent law-breakers but also petty infringements of administrative regulations such as the pass laws. It is, however, imperative to draw a sharp distinction between these two classes of crime because their cause and the nature of the remedy required is quite different. Discussion of African crime will make no real progress unless this distinction is kept in mind continuously.

To clarify the issues it is well first to deal briefly with the hard core of serious crime which consists mainly of violence against persons or of the theft of property or of a combination of both. About a third, or more than 8,000, of the total number of people in prison are recidivists, i.e. men who have been in prison before. This fact in itself suggests that the common belief is false that sending a man to prison will in some wonderful fashion cure him of his criminal ways. It is obvious that our present system of sentencing Natives to long terms of imprisonment is a grim failure. Its main result seems to be to unfit them for life at large and so ensure their early return to prison. No wonder that there is a steady increase in the number of those receiving the indeterminate sentence of seven years after they have already spent some, perhaps many, years in prison.

Since harsh methods have failed, is it not time that we learned the clear lesson that the history of crime teaches, namely, that more humane and enlightened methods of coping with crime are in actual practice more effective than savage and vindictive methods? No doubt the ordinary man will not believe it, but it happens to be true that when the rigours of punishment are relaxed, crime has not increased. It is on that ground, not for reasons of soft sentiment, that the former methods are now advocated in every civilized country.

Not that we can simply leave the matter there. The nature and causes of persistent non-European crime have hitherto received no serious study at all. The legal profession has shown no interest in criminology. Neither the Bench nor the Bar nor the Law Societies in South Africa have ever taken active steps to encourage the study of contemporary crime in either its technical legal or its broader social aspects. Our magistrates have rarely had the advantage of securing that full training or acquiring some knowledge of the social background in the light of which judicial functions can best be discharged. It should be added that the conditions of their appointment and promotion compare very unfavourably with those prevailing in Britain or pre-war France or pre-Hitler Germany.

Our prison visitors' boards are composed mainly of retired magistrates or others who rarely have the capacity to undertake the research required. Yet they are the only people who now have regular access to prisons, records, case histories, and similar material that must form the basis of any scientific inquiry into crime in this country. Pending a planned crime survey of the type so well done in the United States, there is little that can profitably be said about the features of serious crime that are peculiar to South Africa.

79

Petty Offences

The second main type of crime consists of petty offences against laws and regulations having the force of law. These laws are mainly the result of the form of Native administration that has been devised in South Africa. The largest set of these offences arise under the pass laws, the urban areas legislation, and from the attempt to control the consumption of liquor.

It is in this broad field that the major problem emerges. The root of the matter here is that the law is expected to do something which it is far beyond the power of mere law to accomplish. There is in South Africa a deeply rooted tendency to regard law not only as the primary but as the sole agency of social control. This is a fundamental illusion. In no form of society are the laws respected by the common man unless there are also other social forces at work which encourage him to respect the force of law.

In our own European societies these other forces obviously include the home, the family, the school, the neighbourhood, the suburb, as well as the church, the professional or vocational body to which a man belongs, and, not least, the desire to advance in power or wealth since in an acquisitive society none of us is really free from this incentive.

Moreover, we all have some notion of the aims and purposes of the law, especially the criminal law, which we are expected to refrain from breaking. The spectacle of public trials conducted with care and benefit of doubt and a regular procedure encourages in us a high degree of confidence that the police will not bring a charge against us successfully unless there is good or even grave reason for doing so. For us the operations of the criminal law dramatize many of the moral values of the community of which we are members.

Now similar factors were certainly operative in tribal society, a salient feature of which was rigid conformity to law and to the established conventions that were not distinguished from law as we know it. These laws were indeed supported by such a variety of sanctions, direct and indirect, that the Bantu tribesman felt bound to obey them. It was rarely that he resisted this pressure on his mind and conduct.

It is precisely these vital if impalpable factors that are absent from the relation that has now been established between Africans and the law by our present Native policy and by our elaborate network of Native administration. Indeed, nothing measures the magnitude of our failure so clearly as the lawless habits now all too common among a people whose social heritage was marked by such deep respect for law and order.

For even if the police were archangels in blue uniforms, the nature and extent of the petty laws they are now called on to enforce against Africans would alone be enough to create an atmosphere wholly unfavourable to the cultivation of respect for law. To take only the sets of laws and regulations already mentioned—the pass laws, the urban areas legislation, the liquor laws, and the like—these alone constitute an immense range of possible offences, a range so broad that no African can be sure at any time that he is not committing an offence. I make bold to say that the legal position to-day is such that the police can arrest any African walking down the main streets of Johannesburg at any time of the day or night, and any competent prosecutor would have no difficulty whatever in finding *some* offence with which he could be charged.

The fact is that it is impossible for the ordinary African, who cannot even read, let alone understand the language of the laws affecting his daily life and work, to observe all of them. Indeed, if the Natives of South Africa were organized to obey literally all these laws, Native administration and with it the economic life of our country would come to a standstill and those who organized such mass obedience would have to be charged with causing a disturbance !

Of course, many of these laws are not regularly enforced, but they *can* be enforced at any moment. One recalls how easy it was, before the general election in 1943 to arrest 10,000 Natives on the Rand in a month. What we should realize is that even now 2,000 are arrested every week-end, mainly for liquor offences. When this is done; or when the notorious section 17 of the old Urban Areas Act is applied to hundreds of men who are virtually imprisoned without proper trial; or when people are removed without ceremony as illegal tenants from lands they have squatted on for many years, then law loses all meaning or sense for the ordinary man. Moreover, the uncertainty, insecurity, and confusion that results in men's minds infects their whole attitude to law and order, including the criminal law. The very word "law" comes to be associated by them with the opposite implications from those which it has traditionally held and which it still holds for most of us.

It is this current conception of Native administration as a means of attaining certain ends in Native policy that has led directly to the enactment of a wide range of legislation accompanied by an equally wide range of petty offences whose only effective sanction is at present assumed to be imprisonment. We are thus employing the criminal law and the penal system for purposes they were never designed to serve and do not in fact serve in other countries. And by this abuse of means we have gone far to defeat our own end.

Conduct of the Police

As it happens, however, it is quite apparent to even an untrained eye that the police are not archangels in blue uniforms, nor can the criminal law really be regarded as a sure shield designed to protect the property and persons of all races alike from injury or theft. The consequence is that to African eyes the criminal law has no visible merits. They see it not as a shield to protect them but an instrument in the hands of the police to oppress them. If one tries to explain to them the meaning of its underlying principles, such as equality before the law or the rule of law, they will stare incredulously at you and ask how you account for the incident that occurred to a friend last week. You assure them that there is hardly any racial discrimination in our criminal code and its procedure, as passed by Parliament, and they promptly ask you to explain different sentences on black and on white for the same type of offence, or the different attitudes adopted by the police to the two races. In a word the attractive legal theories of the jurist are falsified by the daily administrative practice to which Africans are subjected. The political, administrative, and psychological factors we find in race relations in South Africa are regularly reflected in the operation of the law. Indeed, they are assumed, even by legal administrators, who should know better, to be incidental to the natural order of things. To Africans, however, the vagaries of the legal system are not minor incidents but constitute its most vital aspect. For them the daily discriminations of actual practice make nonsense of the classic claim of the Common law that justice is colour-blind.

They feel themselves caught in a vast network which has little purpose except to punish and humiliate them. The way they received my little pamphlet, *Africans and the Police*—they wrote me innumerable letters about it from all parts of the country—showed me that many even semi-educated men had no idea that they had any rights at all in relation to the police or that the police were themselves subject to law. In this respect my pamphlet was a complete eye-opener ; and I fear that many still believe that I was writing about what the law *ought* to be, not what it is in theory, if not in fact.[1]

The immediate consequence of our readiness to put men in prison on the slightest pretext is to blur the distinction I drew between serious and even heinous crime against one's fellow men on the one hand and on the other mere petty offences against irksome administrative regulations. In our own minds we all recognize this distinction. Parking a car in the wrong place or at the wrong time is an offence known to every motorist ; so is driving so recklessly as to cause a pedestrian injury or

---

[1] The reaction of at least one Native administrator, who was formerly in the police service, is also worth recording. On receiving the pamphlet he promptly ·took it to the police to inquire whether such literature could be freely circulated among those for whom it was intended. I gather that he was informed that it is not a criminal offence to offer to Africans legal advice about their rights even in relation to the police !

death. But everyone knows the immense difference between these two motoring "offences" because, for one thing, our criminal law draws a sharp distinction in the degree of punishment meted out to two such offenders. It sends one to prison for twelve months and fines the other twenty shillings. Now it is just this kind of difference which is absent when we send to the same prison an offender against the pass laws and a homicidal burglar.

It is tempting to suggest that we should reconstruct our whole penal code and its procedure in order to distinguish sharply between serious crime and petty offences.

The great bulk of our criminal law and procedure is based on English law. In the past English law (but not Roman-Dutch law) recognized a considerable difference between felonies or heinous crimes and misdemeanours or petty offences. But the technical difficulties involved as well as the danger of introducing an explicit colour bar in procedure would, I fear, make such a distinction hazardous for our purpose.

It is also tempting to say that the difference between these two types of offences lies in the fact that in serious crime there is an element of moral guilt on the part of the law-breaker and in petty offences there is not. But the temptation to simplify the matter to this extent must be resisted in view of the divided and uncertain view taken by lawyers and courts of the necessity to establish an element of moral guilt in crime.[2]

The fact is that we cannot really count on the lawyers or the courts to detect an element of moral guilt in some crimes and not in others. Where we feel that this difference exists, it is due to our reaction as members of the community in which the offender lives. The courts do usually reflect this feeling in the degree of punishment awarded him. But unfortunately we are not able to devise legal techniques adequate to ensure this desirable result, mainly because circumstances alter cases to an extent that would astonish the inquiring layman.

[2] See J. W. C. Turner's essay on "The Mental Element in Crimes at Common Law" in The Modern Approach to Criminal Law, pp. 195-261 (1945).

Unfortunately, too, a wide range of fines for various degrees of punishment is impossible with people so poor as Africans are. With them a fine of even ten shillings is too much and they must needs accept the alternative of a week in those prisons out of which we want to keep them.

Let us face the fact that there can be no solution of this problem until we recognize that penal sanctions must be abolished for petty offences by Africans against the laws concerned solely with the requirements of Native administration. In any event, it is clear that putting men in prison if they fail to observe the pass laws, the urban areas legislation, or the liquor laws does not in fact help to secure the observance of these laws. Observance of such administrative requirements can be far better secured by depriving a person of certain benefits if he fails to conform to the necessary requirements, *i.e.* by negative obstacles put in his way and not by positive penalty such as imprisonment. If, for instance, we had the labour exchanges we have asked for, then failure to produce a pass would simply handicap an applicant for employment when he comes to the exchange. Or when unemployment insurance benefits are available to him, as they will be in the coming years, he will find that before he can draw them, certain documents of his must be in order.

This is a fundamental truth in Native administration and policy that penal reformers must not only grasp firmly themselves but also seek to hammer into the heads of every administrator and legislator.

Native Law Problems

There is yet a third major consideration that affects the legal order in the eyes of the layman.

With us Europeans the rules of the civil law, being for the most part necessary and sensible, contribute towards our understanding of and respect for the law. But even here Africans receive no real encouragement to try to understand and observe the law.

For it is by no means only the practice of the police and the habits of the courts that seem to illustrate for Africans the perverse and arbitrary nature of law in the society into which we have drawn them.

The recognition and enforcement of Native law and custom has greatly, if quite unexpectedly, added to the prevailing uncertainty in regard to the legal status of the African. The Native Commissioner is endowed with a discretion whether he will apply Native law or Common law to a civil case between Natives. Native law is itself very obscure on many points and we have taken hardly any steps to reduce to writing the tribal customs on which a good deal of Native law depends.

But Native law and custom applies only to cases between Natives. When a Native sues a European or an Indian or a Coloured man, he finds himself under the Common law of the country.

This means that when a black man's cow kills another black man's horse, one law applies ; but when the same black man's same cow kills a white man's horse, a different law applies !

Even in the most important subjects such as the law of inheritance or of guardianship of children, Africans are quite uncertain whether European law or Native custom applies to them.[3] One could cite many instances of the complete lack of that degree of uniformity in applying law to Africans which we Europeans certainly demand and obtain in our own lives.

In addition we have introduced all Africans to the sharp distinction we draw between criminal and civil law, a distinction unknown in tribal life and one which they have been taught only at the point of the police baton. In their own thinking civil and criminal law are still all of a piece. Consequently the weaknesses and confusion apparent in one branch of the law are again carried over to affect their understanding of and reaction to the other branch.

The problems I am now touching on are not all of deliberate

---

[3] *See*, for instance, the draft proclamation in the *Government Gazette*, 19 January, 1945, on inheritance ; and Prentice-Hall law reports, 1944, R. 30 and 1945, H. 121, for cases about a guardian's duty to support a child.

European contrivance, like the pass laws or the urban areas Acts. Some of them are inherent in the legal situation that arises when people are in transition from the tribal to the western way of life. But they are all a part of the legal and social background against which respect for law as such will either grow and flourish or wither and die.

As I see it, a variety of social forces and legal factors—some deep-seated and hard to eradicate, others more superficial and easier to eliminate—have converged to produce the present complex and unhappy position in which Africans find themselves in relation to the law. One thing, however, is as clear as the noonday sun. Respect for law among Africans is dying fast. It is therefore urgent for us to realize that the prevailing instrument of social control in a society may be either law and morals or it may be power and administration. The dominant social trends will move steadily in one direction or the other because in their mature forms such societies are at opposite poles. We have been warned that the steady growth of power and administration at the expense of law and morals will ultimately lead to a form of fascism here as it has done in other countries.[4]

Assuming that we want our society and its public policies to rest on the pillars of law and morals, we must first appreciate the intimate relationship that exists between those twin pillars. It must be emphasized again that that involves recognizing the limits of law alone as an agency of social control. The law can only confirm codes of behaviour that are already observed at least to some degree by reason of the operation of other social forces I mentioned earlier. If this fact were widely appreciated, there would be far better public understanding of the real reasons why Africans break the criminal law. The short-sighted clamour for the law as such to be enforced—when half our administrators and even five per cent. of our legislators know this to be impossible in practice—will slowly subside. In exchange for the dubious ideal of law enforcement, we might accept the ideal of a society based upon laws that really work

[4] *Cf.* E. Bodenheimer : *Jurisprudence* (1940).

because they rest on a moral or at least an obviously sensible basis that commends itself even to the limited understanding of untutored people.

We are therefore brought back to the inescapable fact that the major half of the problem of crime, namely petty offences, is essentially a problem of Native policy. The legislation that creates these innumerable petty offences is the legal reflection of a political attempt to reverse the operation of powerful economic and social forces. This attempt is not only failing in its own purpose but it is also largely responsible for the breakdown of the whole legal order as it affects Africans which is now beginning to threaten us all.

Unless we take early steps to revise radically our Native policy, it will soon be too late to do so effectively. We will have brought into being a large army of lawless and embittered Africans on whose co-operation it will be impossible to count even under a revised system of law and administration. This army threatens to reach its maximum strength and size at a time when the growing trend towards an industrial and urban society in South Africa would in any event result in an increase in crime as it has done all the world over.

Therein lies the gravity of the situation that confronts us. It is a situation that challenges the biggest efforts we can exert because if our efforts are unequal to the task, one trembles to think of the consequences that South Africa will suffer in the years that lie ahead.

8

CRIME AND PUNISHMENT IN AFRICA

THE African tribesman has his own idea of law. To him law is a well-known body of customary rules by which everyone regulates his conduct. There is no clear distinction between criminal and civil law. If one man infringes another's customary rights, a tribal court will hear the case. The court, composed of the Chief assisted by a couple of his councillors, sits in the open under a tree. The parties bring their witnesses and supporters and put their case at great length. Anyone, even passing strangers, can contribute to the discussion, ask a question or make a suggestion to the judges. There are no rules of evidence and nothing will be excluded on the ground of irrelevance. In the end the court will usually award the injured party compensation in the form of a goat or two head of cattle to be paid by the defendant.

Simply to apply English criminal law and procedure to tribes accustomed to such informality is to invite friction and failure. It has therefore been a settled part of British colonial policy, especially in the last twenty years, to recognize Native courts, and their recognition is now a notable feature of the system of "indirect rule". All except the most serious offences or cases to which the Administration attaches special importance, are first tried in these courts which have had conferred on them varying but substantial powers of a kind that they did not have in tribal society. In Tanganyika, for instance, they can imprison for six months or impose a fine of £10; in parts of Uganda they can imprison for twelve months and order a whipping to the extent of twenty-four strokes; and in Nigeria their powers are even wider.

The law administered by Native courts is not English law but Native law and custom "so far as it is not repugnant to natural justice and morality". This customary law is wholly unwritten and hitherto the British Administrations, unlike the French in West Africa, have made no effort to record its substance. An exception is Bechuanaland where the Government took advantage of the presence in the territory of a distinguished anthropologist, Professor I. Schapera, to commission him to compile a *Handbook of Tswana Law and Custom*, which was published in 1938 for the guidance of Native courts and the information of district officers. If a similar project were undertaken in other colonies, with the collaboration of an experienced lawyer, it would greatly benefit the administration of justice according to Native law. Incidentally, the same territory has in its Native Tribunals Proclamation of 1934 made an interesting attempt to develop Native courts on constitutional lines by giving more precision to their structure and personnel.

The recognition of Native law has always been qualified by the proviso that its customs must not be repugnant to our sense of natural justice or morality. Now whatever "morality" may imply, "natural justice" has acquired a distinct significance in English law. It means that anyone acting in a judicial capacity must observe certain minimum rules of procedure and evidence, which have been authoritatively declared to be at least three in number. Firstly, a man may not be a judge in his own cause ; the judicial mind must be free from all considerations of self-interest. Secondly, no party ought to be condemned unheard. The defendant must know in good time the case he has to meet and he must be given ample opportunity to answer it. Thirdly, when an appeal is decided, the court should state the reasons for its decision. It need hardly be added that every court is under a duty to decide the case before it according to the evidence.

Yet, curiously enough, we have made no attempt in British Africa to get Native courts to appreciate the value of these elementary principles of justice. A Native chief has been known to hear his own divorce case. Judges who have themselves heard none of the evidence have passed sentence of six months' imprisonment. Occasionally corruption, always very difficult to detect, has been found among Native judges, as it was just lately in Nigeria. In such cases the district officer (or, more rarely, the High Court) takes action, but over the thousands of cases heard, his supervision, amid many administrative duties, must needs be perfunctory.

A practical difficulty in supervising the work of subordinate courts is the lack of adequate records. Every court should be encouraged and, wherever possible, compelled to keep some record, however sketchy, of its proceedings. Some colonies have begun to do so, but the records usually include only the names of the parties, the nature of the charge and the sentence. If the district officer's supervision is to be effective, these details should be amplified. A set of model records might be drawn up and widely circulated. Moreover, young Africans could be specially trained to serve as clerks to tribal courts. Above all, it would be of real educational value if, while preserving their natural informality, we were to lay down a few simple general principles to guide their procedure. We can surely maintain the standards of British justice without applying either the substance of English law or the full rigour of its rules of evidence and procedure.

The punishments imposed by Native courts are another aspect of their work that awaits attention. Imprisonment was not a form of punishment known to the Africans. Europeans introduced them to it and they have not been slow to adopt it where they can in their own local administration. In place of the compensation normally awarded an injured party in tribal law, Native courts may now imprison a culprit. Where Native authorities establish their own prisons, as in Nigeria and Uganda, a full prison comes to be regarded as a sign of the chief's power and status. But imprisonment is not associated mainly with Native courts. When the district officer, or, in the towns, a magistrate convicts an offender in a serious case, imprisonment is the usual sentence. The option of a fine is too seldom exercised because, the average yearly income in cash of an African being less than £5, even 10s. is too large a sum to pay. Nor is it only the serious offenders who are sent to prison. In colonies like Kenya and Southern Rhodesia there are thousands of Africans in prison for short terms because they were guilty of merely technical offences such as failure to carry a pass, or cutting down forest trees, or polluting a stream. Imprisonment as a deterrent is falling out of favour in England. Of what use is it in Africa? No social stigma attaches to the African who has been to prison. He has simply had another adventure that has brought him no nearer an understanding of the white man's strange customs. On his return he will tell his astonished friends how the warder put him in a room of his own, fed him regularly, gave him a uniform to wear and sometimes even began to teach him a trade. No wonder that a director of prisons can complain that during the depression Africans committed minor offences in order to obtain refuge from the vagaries of life at large ; or that an African convict, accidentally shut out of the prison at night, will clamour for admission ; or that an anthropologist recently reported ambitious fathers to be consulting the district officer as to what crime their son had better commit so as to get enough time in prison to be able to benefit by the training there given.

Not that prisons in Africa are such delightful places. Those who have inspected them in the light of modern standards can tell grim stories. "The actual jail accommodation," writes one not given to exaggeration, "is primitive and unsuitable in the great majority of cases ; the treatment of prisoners can make little claim to be methodical or scientific ; and the whole system is little better than a primitive effort at punishment which largely fails even as a deterrent."[1] There are few reformatories and those that exist must serve an enormous area. It must, however, be added that the immense distances in Africa, the sparse population, and the poor transport make the problem

[1] Major G. St. J. Orde Browne in an article on "The African Prisoner" in the *Contemporary Review*, May, 1937.

of prisons hard to tackle even where there is a desire to do so, while the absence of social services and welfare agencies renders the task of constructive effort doubly difficult.

If prison is a dubious agency to reform or deter, is corporal punishment the alternative? Among both European settlers and many lawyers in Africa there is a strong belief that whipping or the lash is the only language that Native law-breakers really understand. It will be hard to shake this belief even though the evidence in its favour must be very meagre. One can only cite the unanimous conclusion reached by the Bushe Commission on criminal justice in East Africa: "the punishments sanctioned by all enlightened systems of jurisprudence are the most suitable for these territories."[2] It is a pity that lawyers in the colonial service and the district officers, on whom so much depends, are seldom well-informed about modern methods of coping with crime or of treating criminals.

District officers who try the majority of serious cases lack a legal training and they are hardly ever well enough versed in jurisprudence to be able confidently to adapt ancient law to novel circumstances that were not contemplated by the writers of standard text-books. The principles of criminal liability, for example, are not the most up-to-date or scientific branch of English law, but they have been embodied in the penal codes that are applied in the colonies. Now questions of motive, intention, good faith and, above all, provocation in the mind of a primitive African cannot be judged as if an ordinary Englishman were in the dock. Yet the remarkable decision by the Court of Appeal in South Africa (which also affects Southern Rhodesia) in *Mbombela's* case shows how inflexibly it is possible to interpret criminal law. In that case, an African, acting under the widespread and profound belief prevailing in his territory that a deadly evil spirit assumes the form of a dwarf with small feet, struck with an hatchet at such a figure which he saw in an ill-lit hut. In fact he killed a child who was his own nephew. Now to constitue a defence in criminal law, a mistaken belief

[2] Cmd. 4623 (1934), para. 164.

93

must be a reasonable one. In deciding whether a mistake of fact is reasonable, the standard is that of a fictitious legal figure, "the reasonable man". The Court of Appeal held that "the race, idiosyncracies, superstitions or intelligence of the accused do not enter into the question".[3]

With this curious judgment may be contrasted the wise recommendation of the Bushe Commission which considered a similar point. The report[4] reminds us that in England an accused person always has the benefit of trial by jury. This ensures that when a question such as the degree of provocation suffered by an ordinary person in certain circumstances has to be decided, it will be decided by twelve people whose emotions resemble those of the accused. In a colonial court, however, an Englishman is trying an African and in such a trial it is important that the conception of "an ordinary person" should be that of the tribal community to which the accused belongs. If almost any tribesman would have struck a blow when acting under the influence of the common belief in witchcraft, it is no matter that the Englishman on the bench would have remained unmoved!

This illustration must suffice to indicate the perplexities that result from the contact and conflict of two races with two different legal systems. To assist the courts in their solution, the appointment of public defenders, as proposed by the Bushe Commission and subsequently endorsed by the conference of East African Governors, is a means that should not be neglected any longer. Finally, if we could at least give the colonial cadets in training at Oxford and Cambridge a smattering of sociological jurisprudence, we should be entitled to expect both criminal justice and penal reform in Africa to make some progress in the coming years.

[3] R. v. Mbombela, 1933, A.D. 269.
[4] Para. 212.

9

NATIVE COURTS AND

BRITISH JUSTICE IN AFRICA

FOR many years now Native courts have been a feature of colonial administration in British Africa. They are to be found in almost every district and they hear thousands of cases. Yet such is the confusion of thought that exists about their aims and functions that these courts have not yet made anything like the contribution to our knowledge of Native law that might have been expected.

In the first place it is necessary to emphasize the distinction, recognized by lawyers but often ignored by laymen, between a court and the body of law it applies to the case before it. In South Africa, for instance, a Native Commissioner's Court, in which the man on the bench is always a European, has power to apply either Native law or European law, *i.e.* the Common law.[1] In the Union there are also hundreds of Chief's courts which have power to apply only Native law. Only recognized Chiefs sit in these courts, which correspond roughly to the Native courts familiar in British Africa.

In both sets of courts in the Union, the body of law to be applied is specifically mentioned in the governing statute. The Chief has no option but to apply Native law; but the Native Commissioner can exercise his discretion whether to apply Native law or the Common law, provided that he decides

[1] Lawyers know no body of law by the name of 'European law'. In South Africa European law means the Roman-Dutch law which is the Common law of the country and which has now come to be called 'South African law'. In British Africa European law means the English Common law. For the sake of clarity, as well as convenience, I shall refer to European law, whether in the Union or in British Africa, as 'the Common law' This is really a better term because the body of law indicated often applies to Africans and Europeans alike.

which it is that he is applying and that his decision is clear from the written record of the case. The way in which this discretion has been exercised in a particular case is often a ground of appeal to the Native Appeal Court, which is also staffed by Europeans, and which can reverse the Native Commissioner's decision. In other words, the court for cases between Natives will not necessarily apply Native law unless it is a Chief's court, which must do so.

Native courts in British Africa were, of course, originally established in order to administer justice according to Native law and custom. This policy was based on the belief that Natives would know Native law better than Europeans could know it so the work had much better be left to them. No doubt there was much to justify this view twenty years ago. But the question we should be asking now is whether this policy was designed to take sufficient account of changing circumstances and, more particularly, whether it was and is calculated to encourage the growth of *a system of Native law*.[2] Has British policy in the past not shown too much concern for Native courts and too little for Native law?

This weakness is suggested by the fact that although thousands of Native courts have been applying Native law for many years, we all know little more now about the substance of Native law, as distinct from the general background of Native life, than we did when these courts were first set up. The reason is not hard to find. In no colony, with the exception of Bechuanaland, have serious efforts been made to reduce Native law to writing, or at least to take the first big step in this direction, by not only keeping, but also publishing, adequate records of the cases actually heard in Native courts. Yet this is both the obvious and the traditional way in which the development of a body of law is fostered wherever the legal system is based on the theory of precedent.

[2] By a legal system is implied a body of rules which are related by consistency and coherence and from which further rules can be drawn by inference or extended by analogy.

"The bare outline of this theory is easy enough to sketch," says a modern writer on English law. "Resting as it does upon the authority of judicial decisions, it is necessarily dependent upon the existence of a regular and satisfactory series of reports in which this authority may be enshrined. It is not surprising, therefore, that the theory emerges with the first printed reports of the sixteenth century and that it is elaborated on the appearance of the semi-official reports of the nineteenth. For the same reason the county and police courts, whose judgments are not reported, play no part in the development of the theory."[3]

Usually, as with the Common law, whether in England or in South Africa, the higher courts apply the same body of law as the lower courts from which appeals reach them. It is then only the decisions of the higher courts that are recorded and published in the form of regular law reports. These reports are then available to the lower courts, which are in future bound by them. They are also referred to by the higher courts themselves, which will attach more or less authority to them according to the degree to which the theory of precedent is entrenched in the system.

The position in Africa is peculiar because it is the reverse of the usual relationship under which the lower courts are guided by the higher, where rests the real responsibility for developing the theory, doctrines, or positive rules that are the foundation of the whole system. In Africa the British are—almost unconsciously, it seems—trying to build up a system of Native law with materials supplied from below, and only to a small extent with guidance coming from the higher courts above. A certain amount of guidance must necessarily come from the High Courts, which, however rarely, do sometimes hear appeals involving questions of the substance and the practice of Native law. This fact also explains why we are inevitably imposing on Native Africa a system of law based on precedent. The reason is that the system of law originally introduced into, and now in force in, the British colonies is English law. When we recognized

[3] C. H. S. Fifoot, *English Law and Its Background*, (1932), p. 24.

Native law to some uncertain extent by setting up Native courts, it was on the inarticulate assumption that Native law would somehow fit into the framework already established for the purpose of constitutional government and the rule of law.

There is no need to regret this fact if it is considered in its proper perspective. English law provides the basis and the framework of the whole legal system. This does not mean that Native law should not be applied in its own limited sphere. But it does mean that the extent and the method of its application are matters to be determined (as in fact they now are) by the rules and doctrines of English law. Failure by administrators to apprehend this position has been responsible for much of the *laissez faire* policy adopted towards Native courts. This policy has left the Native courts without sufficient direction, particularly in the important field of procedure, from any source but the High Court—if an occasional reversal of a decision can be called direction when it may never even be communicated to the Native court!

Why, it may be asked, should the High Court upset a decision of a Native court on a matter of procedure? The answer is that there are certain rules of procedure so fundamental in any system of law that their observance is obligatory on every court of law. These rules are known to lawyers as "the principles of natural justice", and it must be remembered that Britain always undertook to respect Native law and custom only so far as it is not repugnant to natural justice.[4]

It is difficult to define completely what is meant by natural justice. The phrase is employed to denote a few elementary principles which, according to English ideas, must be followed by all who discharge judicial functions. It has been authoritatively said that these principles "are implicit in the rule of law and that their observance is demanded by our national sense of justice."[5] They are, indeed, the essence of British justice, which

---

[4] Cf. my article in the *Journal of Comparative Legislation and International Law*, 1938.

[5] *Report of the Committee on Ministers' Powers*, Cmd. 4060, 1932, p. 7.

is the pride of Englishmen at home but which they have been slow to plant abroad. Thus it is contrary to natural justice to arrive at a decision before both parties have had an opportunity of stating their case, because no one must be condemned unheard. Another principle is that the judges must have no personal interest in the outcome of the case. A third is that they must all hear all the evidence presented.[6]

Insistence on respect for the principles of natural justice does not mean that we want to impose on a Native court the full formality and rigour of the English law of evidence or procedure. It does mean, however, that the elementary concepts of British justice are a part of the essentials of civilization that we bring to Africa along with vaccination and drains and literacy.

There is another major reason why Native courts cannot be left to act merely in accordance with traditional law and custom. The cases they hear nowadays are not concerned solely with tribal law. Natives are doing all sorts of things, such as trading and adopting new methods of agriculture, for which there is no precedent in Native law.

Lord Hailey drew attention to this fact :

"In old times the types of cases heard before the chief's or tribal court were limited to sexual or agricultural affairs, inheritances, witchcraft, and other matters which often concerned a narrow circle only, and were ruled by well-known conventions and hardly affected by circumstances outside the tribal control. To-day Native society is more complicated and feels itself dependent on an alien rule and on economic and social conditions over which it has no control. The Native Authority and the Native court have become increasingly concerned with the problems arising out of the impact of the new conditions on tribal society."[7]

However well versed a chief or his counsellors may be in the old Native law, are they able, without proper guidance, to

---

[6] Africans are not accustomed to these rules. *See*, for instance, the Law Reports of the West African Court of Appeal, 1936-7, Vol. III, p. 55.

[7] *An African Survey* (1938), p. 303.

extend old rules by analogy or otherwise, to the new situations? And, if they really are, the need to record these new extensions and developments in Native law, both for our information and for exposition to all the people concerned, is even stronger.

The necessity of keeping Native law abreast of changing social conditions has been appreciated in one or two colonies. An attempt to meet it has been made in Uganda by the appointment of a "Judicial Adviser", whose function is described as that of "guide, philosopher, and friend" to the Native courts. A recent Committee of Enquiry into Native Tribunals in the Gold Coast recommended a similar appointment for that colony:

"The functions of the Judicial Adviser would be, *inter alia*, to advise Native Authorities in regard to the improvement of the administration of justice in their courts by the preparation of model rules of court dealing with such matters as court procedure, evidence, and the like. He would also suggest to State Councils subjects about which they might usefully make declarations and modifications of customary law and would revise drafts of such declarations. He would be the final authority for reviewing decisions of Native tribunals and would be director of the training course for registrars. Lastly, he would be a link between the Native courts, the Executive, and the Judiciary."[8]

Whether a single person as Judicial Adviser is the best expedient for dealing with the problems that have arisen is doubtful. But as the relations of courts, law, and legislative bodies become fully understood and operative, there should be no need for such an officer. The local Native Authority should be encouraged, as it is in Tanganyika, to make laws on any subject within its defined powers. These local laws are in effect regulations or bye-laws made under an enabling statute. Their place in a legal system and the method of interpreting them adopted by courts would be broadly the same as it is in the English legal system.

The same paragraph of the Report referred to illustrates the present confusion. A certain Native court, it tells us, recently

[8] *Report of the Native Tribunals Committee of Enquiry, Accra, 1943, para. 23.*

decided that the fee (*i.e.* fine or damages payable) for the seduction of a schoolgirl should be higher than that imposed in the case of an uneducated girl on the ground that her parents had spent more on her—notwithstanding that under Native custom there is a fixed fee. "It is, however, doubtful," says the Committee, "whether an appeal court would uphold this decision." If that is so, the obvious solution is to embody the new rule, allowing higher damages to be awarded in such cases, in a regulation or bye-law, *i.e.* to pass local legislation which every court must accept and apply. It may be noted, incidentally, that in South Africa in precisely the same kind of case higher damages have been allowed by the Native Appeal Courts in the exercise of their judicial discretion. Sometimes, but not always, they interpret their function so as to include the adaptation of Native law in suitable cases, thus rendering new legislation unnecessary. Where, however, the courts take a rigid view of the judicial process, adaptation must be accomplished by legislation, just as it often is in the English legal system.

What is the future of Native courts? It is certain that as African life grows more diversified and more highly specialized, as its social and economic level is raised—and it is now the declared policy of Britain to raise it—the nature of the cases coming before Native courts will reflect these changes. Traditional tribal law and custom will be found less and less able to cope with problems wholly new to, and different from, its familiar conceptions. Legal history has, of course, known plenty of parallels to this situation and it is full of the fictions and strategies that adjustment has rendered necessary. If the work of Native courts is not to suffer under this strain, we should take active steps to prepare them for it.

In the first place the time is overdue for the recording of Native law. The best way to approach this task would be to collect, collate, and publish such records of cases heard in Native courts as are already available in district offices and elsewhere. Until this is done, Native law cannot receive the benefit of serious study and discussion by independent specialists outside the local administration. Such study and discussion is essential to the healthy growth of any body of law.

Recording will also facilitate the second main task, which is the unification of Native law, at least in wide areas where social and economic conditions make it desirable. No doubt we can hardly hope soon to secure a Native Common law in colonies where scores if not hundreds of tribes each cherish their own traditions. Yet South African experience suggests that the obstacles are often exaggerated, especially in the field of marriage and inheritance which still covers a large proportion of the cases. At least we should have clear and conscious aims and a policy that will steadily approach them. The Common law of England would have been a much longer time emerging, and the national consciousness much slower to develop, if Henry II had not imposed a certain measure of uniformity by insisting that royal justice should compete with, if not replace, local custom. Not only political growth but also economic expediency point in this direction. Internal trade by Natives will find itself hampered by the lack of a legal system that provides the essential conditions of commercial security.

How far Native law itself can be developed for this purpose is a doubtful question. The higher courts are tending to rely more and more on English law, a tendency that is natural and inevitable in all the circumstances. It should, however, be possible to simplify English law by local legislation and possibly even to harmonize it to some extent with a dynamic body of Native law. But these fruitful possibilities demand an energetic policy towards Native law in contrast to the negative attitude that has hitherto prevailed. English lawyers at home are on the whole a rather backward race, who shrink from innovation and, indeed, from conscious law-making of almost any description. Let us hope that they may yet respond to the challenge to fresh thinking that Africa offers in every field of work.

10

THE RECOGNITION

OF AFRICAN NATIVE LAW

THE reconstruction of Africa is not the least of the tasks that awaits the world's attention. A part of this task is certainly the revision of the policy adopted by various African territories in regard to Native law. The purpose of this essay is to suggest the major legal questions that British policy will find itself faced with. Some if not all of these questions have already arisen in the Union of South Africa, whose experience furnishes in many respects a useful guide both to what might be done and what might be avoided. The Union is the oldest and strongest State in all Africa, with a longer history and a more varied experience of Native policy, including Native law, than any other part of the continent south of the Sahara.

A desire to respect Native law and to apply it where possible is common to all the colonial governments in Africa. During the last half-century many enabling statutes have testified to this desire.[1] These statutes were almost invariably drafted in a permissive form which gave the courts discretionary power to apply Native law to the settlement of a case between Natives.

The first problem presents itself here. "Native law and custom" is a common enough phrase, but it is not a precise indication of a body of law applied to a particular case in the sense that English or Roman-Dutch or even Hindu or Mohammedan law can be applied. The reason is that there is no one body of Native law in Africa or even in any large region. There are innumerable Native tribes scattered all over the continent and varying in number from a few hundred people to a million

---

[1] For the references, *see* my article in *Journal of Comparative Legislation and International Law*, Vol. XX, pp. 16-23 (1938).

or more. Each of these tribes may be described as having its own body of customary law. Some tribes and their laws are related to and resemble their neighbours or other tribes further afield, but often enough neighbouring tribes are ethnically different and culturally distinct, and they also speak unrelated languages. Moreover, these tribal differences by no means correspond with the international boundaries drawn on the maps. A tribal map of Africa shows surprising departures from the political map that one normally looks at. There is hardly a single political frontier which does not cut across tribal divisions in a quite ruthless fashion. The map was drawn in the course of the scramble for Africa in the late nineteenth century, when no one cared, if anyone knew, about nice anthropological differences.

Africans were all illiterate before the white man came. There were consequently no records whatever of their customary law, and it is a matter for regret that European governments have on the whole been so slow to record Native law. Some progress has been made in this direction in South Africa, but even there the purposeful Victorian interest in the subject did not persist into the twentieth century. In British West and East Africa virtually nothing has been attempted and the literature on Native law is of the most meagre kind. If British policy really aims to apply Native law and to assure its preservation for the future, it must take steps to reduce to writing at least those customs which are the cause of regular litigation. It is hardly necessary to add that the recording of Native law need not mean petrifying it. Handbooks are not codes, but if their publication encourages a movement towards codification, the case for codification will have become so strong by that time as to deserve careful consideration.

The better the substance of Native law in any area is known, the larger will the next difficulty loom. This is the question of the conflict of Native law with English law (or whatever Common law was originally introduced by the European power). European law is the foundation on which constitutional government rests in Africa. It has also supplied the law of crime, of commerce, of property, and of procedure, as these are branches of law in which Native custom cannot provide rules since they reflect phenomena unknown in Native life. Native law is, however, not something utterly different from European law. Native law is essentially family or personal law, and many of its commonest institutions and categories are the same as or at least similar to those found in European law. Thus there is a Native law of marriage and divorce, of marriage contracts or settlements or dowry, of seduction, of illegitimacy and the adoption of children, of guardianship, of torts, and of inheritance. In all these categories the Native law is, indeed, as one would expect, not as well worked out, nor its concepts as refined, as the comparable rules of European law. Whether it is capable of development to meet the unforeseen circumstances of modern African life is a doubtful question. What really matters, however, is not whether such a development is possible, but whether it is desirable on lines different from or parallel to the European law.

A single example will illustrate the issue. The action for seduction is very common in South Africa. In Native law, as in English law, the father or guardian of the woman seduced brings the action, but he can bring it either against the seducer or against his *kraalhead*, *i.e.*, the head of the collective household to which the seducer belongs, or against both jointly. In Roman-Dutch law, however (which is the Common law of the country), the woman herself, if she is not a minor, brings the action, and only against her seducer. Where statute enjoins the court to apply Native law where it will best serve the interests of justice, must the court insist on the woman's father bringing the action? Must it do so even where the woman lives in another province from her father and no longer under tribal conditions but as a free individual? In other words, does the intention to apply Native law deprive a litigant of her rights under the Common law? If, on the other hand, she exercises

105

those rights, does her action deprive her father of his rights under Native law?

These questions arise from the uncertain relation of Native law to European law in Africa. It is a problem that has hardly arisen elsewhere in this form. In India, for instance, or in Palestine, where a body of non-European law has been recognized, the basis of its recognition has been the religious community of its adherents. In such circumstances it would be the rare exception, not the normal rule, for a litigant to have combined in his conduct elements of two different systems of family law. One would not expect to find that Hindus or Jews had, while maintaining their traditional habits, also adopted a certain custom from Mohammedan or English law. No doubt provision is made for the man who does not care to be counted a Hindu or a Jew. He in effect contracts out of his religious community and then falls under English law, just as the resident Englishman does.

But the recognition of Native law in Africa cannot be put on a similar basis except, of course, where, as in parts of Nigeria, Mohammedan law is entrenched. African Native law means the immemorial customs of local groups. In some respects these customs are tough and tenaciously observed; but in other respects they are fragile and easily abandoned or drastically modified under the pressure of European influence. The law of marriage illustrates a common problem here. An African can marry by Christian rites, *i.e.*, under the Common law, as no Hindu in India would normally do. When an African chooses to do so, to what extent does he abandon his duties under Native law, particularly where by doing so he would deprive a third party of certain rights? Thus a marriage by Native law is usually validated by the gift of cattle which passes from the bridegroom (or his father) to the father of the bride. If an adult bride and bridegroom choose to marry under the Common law, can the bride's father claim the cattle due to him under Native law? If he does so after the marriage, and the husband refuses to pay them, is the wife justified in deserting him on the ground that he has made the marriage intolerable by his refusal to meet her father's claim?[2]

Second only to the conflict of Native and European law is the conflict that occurs between the various bodies of tribal laws. Cases involving such conflicts have increased through the migration of Native labour which now takes place on a large scale. African men attracted by the work and wages offered by mining industries and other forms of economic enterprise, are travelling long distances from their homes. In all the bigger centres of Southern, Eastern, and West Africa there is to-day much inter-tribal mingling of races. On the Witwatersrand and on the copper belt of Rhodesia it is certainly true, as it was in medieval times, that "five men, each under different personal law, may be found walking or sitting together."

There is yet another complication. The customs recognized as Native law are ancient ones. But in actual fact many of these customs, or certain features of them, are changing as the social and economic conditions of Native life change. Nowhere in the world has social change been as swift and as far-reaching as it has in Africa in the last two or three decades. Where customs of marriage or family life have undergone significant change, which form of the custom shall the courts recognize as Native law? Shall they countenance only the practice of the oldest generation? Or shall they seek to find current or contemporary custom in the practice of younger people? They will probably be tempted, as in South Africa, to do the first. If they do, they can, where necessary, use well-established legal methods of recognizing a local custom as law.[3] But they will thereby run the risk of making law equivalent in the eyes of the younger generation to old-fashioned and out-moded custom, if not to

[2] The psychological factor is important. Without any understanding of the legal issues, most Native women in South Africa would feel themselves not properly married unless cattle or their equivalent had been paid. The question has arisen more than once in South African courts, and there are now conflicting decisions.

[3] I discussed the ways of proving a custom in my article in the *Journal of Comparative Legislation and International Law* in 1938.

vested interest in the vanishing past. It is harder for the courts to choose on occasion the second alternative and recognize changes in custom. If they do, however, they might well adopt the tests which English and South African courts apply before they uphold as law trade usages, such as the practices of stock-brokers or auctioneers, which are a form of modern mercantile custom.

Marriage is the central institution around which Native law revolves. The majority of Natives marry according to Native law or custom, but the number who marry by Christian rites under the Common law was never negligible, and it is growing fairly rapidly. In the old Cape Colony marriages by Native law were refused recognition. The judges have been severely criti-cized for this refusal by administrators and anthropologists who believed that it was due to judicial ignorance of the part played in Native marriage by the transfer of cattle. Closer inquiry, however, discloses the fact that the reason for the refusal to recognize Native marriages was not simply a mistaken belief that they involved purchase and sale of the woman. The main reason was that the Legislature had not at that time empowered the courts to recognize Native law, and consequently they had no power to recognize Native marriage which was an integral part of Native law. In these circumstances the courts really had no option but to regard the transfer of cattle as consideration offered for the immoral purpose of cohabitation with a woman, and they accordingly declined to enforce such contracts or rights that arose out of them. No doubt there are cases on record in which the judges displayed a Victorian aversion from any other form of marriage or morals than that to which they were themselves accustomed. But, at least equally, there are cases on record in which the judges showed as penetrating an insight into Native custom as any anthropologist.[4] What led them to decide against recognition were rules contained in an

---

[4] *See*, for instance, the remarkable judgment of Mr. Justice S. T. Jones in *Nbono v. Manoxoweni*, 1891, *Eastern Districts Courts Law Reports*, Vol. VI, pp. 62-99. Another case is reported in 1 E.D.C. 195 (1880).

established part of the Common law which they were bound to uphold. These rules are still part of the Common law, although now, as in the nineteenth century, judicial opinions differ about the way to interpret or enforce them in any particular case.[5]

Nor does the recognition of Native law settle the matter. When South Africa belatedly recognized Native law in 1927, recognition took the usual form of authorizing the court to apply Native custom where it thought fit. At the same time it was expressly stated in the statute that *lobolo* or cattle-dowry cases were not to be refused a hearing on the ground that the custom was repugnant to morality.[6] It is significant of the recurrent failure to foresee the main problems in recognizing Native law that this statute, though designed to make reparation for the thoughtless past, itself failed to define the vital relation of marriage by Native law to marriage under Common law. For it is not enough for the Legislature to recognize the Native form of marriage. Having regard to the known tendency of Natives to combine European and Native habits of life, it is essential for lawyers to know whether a Native already married by Native law can marry another woman under Common law without being divorced. South Africa finally settled this question by an amending Act in 1929, which made clear the relation between the two forms of marriage. A man who is married under the Common law cannot, during the subsistence of his marriage, contract a valid "customary union", as marriages by Native law are now called.[7] The same principle has been adopted by legislation in most of the British colonies in Africa.[8] But neither in the Union nor in British Africa has legislation yet clarified the position of a man who, being married by Native law, proceeds to marry another woman under the Common law. It is assumed in practice in the Union that the first marriage is dissolved by the second ; but it is hard to say what rights, especially

[5] Cf. *Harvard Law Review*, Vol. LIV, pp. 473-482 (1940-41) on Marriage, Contracts, and Public Policy.

[6] Native Administration Act, No. 38 of 1927, s. 11.

[7] Act No. 9 of 1929, s. 9.

[8] For the references, *see* the fourth essay in this book.

of inheritance, remain to the wives and children of the first marriage, which would often have been polygamous. This situation is not simplified by the lack of registration (except in the Province of Natal) of both marriage and divorce by Native law.[9]

Linked with marriage is the law of inheritance. Although Africans marry readily enough under the Common law, they would normally prefer that their property should be inherited not according to European law but according to the customary rules of Native law. This desire was recognized in the old Cape Colony by statute as long ago as 1864,[10] and it has also been respected by the Union.[11] But the practical difficulties encountered in the administration of such a law have been considerable. For one thing, under Native law women do not inherit under any circumstances. Yet in these modern days when a man and wife have married under the Common law and lived as Christians, probably quite apart from his relatives, the widow is not content to allow all her deceased husband's property to pass to his brother or some more remote male relative, even though this successor is in Native law under an obligation to support her if she agrees to live with his household group. Cases of obvious hardship are regularly reported and they have given rise to a demand for some alteration in the present law.[12] Africans in the Union are by statute entitled to make wills,[13] and a slowly increasing number of them do so with the assistance of solicitors. The root of the problem here, however, is uncertainty about how far the normal incidents and consequences of a Christian marriage under the Common law should be attached to Africans who contract such a marriage rather

[9] The essential elements in marriage and the grounds of divorce under the main branches of Native law in South Africa are described in the third essay in this book.

[10] Native Succession Act, No. 18 of 1864.

[11] Native Administration Act, 1927, s. 23, and Regulations issued in the form of Government Notice No. 1664 of September 20, 1929.

[12] See the discussion in the Native Representative Council, 1940, reported in Proceedings, Vol. II, pp. 287-296.

[13] Native Administration Act, 1927, s. 23 (3).

for religious reasons than because they intend to put themselves wholly under European law.

The contact and conflict of two different systems of family law within one country is bound to produce social and legal problems of an intricate kind. South Africa's century of experience provides ample evidence of this fact. If the British dependencies in Africa have not yet had to meet the full range of these problems, it is mainly because, under the policy of indirect rule, the great bulk of litigation between Africans has been left for disposal by Native courts with only the most perfunctory supervision by British administrative officers, who are usually men without a full legal training. To-day civil cases from these courts rarely reach the High Courts, whose decisions alone are published. But as Africans are drawn more and more into the European economic system, and as they rise in the economic scale, their desire and ability to take cases on appeal from the lower courts will increase, as it has done in the Union, and there will always be lawyers at hand to encourage this desire. It is therefore unlikely that British Africa will be spared the necessity of facing the legal problems that have already confronted the Union.

The obvious way of solving some of the problems indicated is by legislation. Hitherto, however, an alien government has shrunk from the task of regulating by law the domestic customs of its subjects. It has preferred to leave the effort to the vagaries of judicial decision, which is less open to popular criticism. But such a policy is exposed to another danger, one that has shown itself recently in South Africa. Free to develop Native law, the Native Appeal Court (which is manned by European judges) has allowed some important decisions to be influenced by an avowed anxiety to pursue a policy of "legal segregation" in harmony with the general policy of political, social, and economic segregation of Africans that has hitherto prevailed in the country. Almost unobserved, it has tried to turn away from the old Cape objective of assimilating Native and European law into one common legal system. How far it will succeed in this

111

departure from earlier tradition it is too early to say. But the mere attempt illustrates the wisdom of the warning on this subject that Macaulay issued to his countrymen more than a century ago.[14]

In urging the need for codification in India, Macaulay pointed out that the state of the indigenous law was such that the alternative was to let "everything depend on the temper of the individual judge."

"Even in this country," he said, "we have had complaints of judge-made law; even in this country, where the state of morality is higher than in almost any other part of the world; where, during several generations, not one depositary of our legal traditions has incurred the suspicion of personal corruption; where there are popular institutions; where every decision is watched by a shrewd and learned audience; where there is an intelligent and observant public; where every remarkable case is fully reported in a hundred newspapers; where, in short, there is everything which can mitigate the evils of such a system. But judge-made law, where there is an absolute government and lax morality, where there is no Bar and no public, is a curse and a scandal not to be endured."

Macaulay went on to explain that he did "not mean that all the people of India should live under the same law: far from it. . . . We know how desirable that object is; but we also know that it is unattainable. We know that respect must be paid to feelings generated by differences of religion, of nation, of caste. Much, I am persuaded, may be done to assimilate the different systems of law without wounding those feelings. But, whether we assimilate those systems or not, let us ascertain them; let us digest them. We propose no rash innovation; we wish to give no shock to the prejudices of any part of our subjects. Our principle is simply this: uniformity where you can have it; diversity where you must have it; but in all cases certainty."

Macaulay supported his plea by another argument. He believed

[14] See his speech on the Government of India in the House of Commons, July 10, 1833. It is in *Selected Speeches*, edited by G. M. Young (1935).

that "a code is almost the only blessing, perhaps it is the only blessing, which absolute governments are better fitted to confer on a nation than popular governments. The work of digesting a vast and artificial system of unwritten jurisprudence is far more easily performed, and far better performed, by a few minds than by many, by a Napoleon than by a Chamber of Deputies and a Chamber of Peers, by a government like that of Prussia or Denmark than by a government like that of England. A quiet knot of two or three veteran jurists is an infinitely better machinery for such purpose than a large popular assembly divided, as such assemblies almost always are, into diverse factions. This seems to me, therefore, to be precisely that point of time at which the advantage of a completely written code of laws may be most easily conferred on India. It is a work which cannot well be performed in an age of barbarism, which cannot without great difficulty be performed in an age of freedom. It is a work which especially belongs to a government like that of India, to an enlightened and paternal despotism."

Macaulay's speech and his political influence accomplished his purpose. In the latter half of the nineteenth century four Law Commissions visited India in order to advise on the codification of its laws. The personnel of these Commissions included men like Macaulay, Lord Romilly, Mr. Justice Willis, and Mr. Justice Lush, while Maine and Fitzjames Stephen also shaped policy as law members of the Viceroy's Council. The task was, however, never fully completed. But no one doubts that the laws of India are much the better for the effort inspired by Macaulay. In Africa the obstacles to such reform are considerably less than they were in India, mainly because Native laws are not fortified, as in India, by strong religious feelings. The recording and unification of Native laws and customs over wide areas is a project that should not be delayed any longer. What Britain did for India in the nineteenth century is the least she can do for Africa in the twentieth.

11

SOME LOBOLO CASES

South Africa has a unique series of law reports devoted to the recording of cases between Natives in which Native law was applied. This important and valuable source of our knowledge of Native law has been neglected in the past. No doubt one reason for this neglect has been the fact that the reports, especially the older ones, were relatively inaccessible; and another reason may well be the difficulties that their technical language and tacit assumptions often present to the inquirer who is not a lawyer.

With a view to making at least the nature of these reports better known, I have selected for reproduction here a series of cases heard in the Native Appeal Courts on various subjects, and I have added explanatory notes to help the layman to notice features of special interest to students of Native law.

Matende Mncube v. Komolo Mazibuko 1941, N.A.C. (Natal and Transvaal) 14

This case turns on the rule that a Native who is a party to a marriage under the Common law, cannot while his marriage continues, become a party to a customary union under Native law. If he purports to enter such a union, it has no legal validity. Moreover, where, as in this case, he pays cattle in contemplation of such a union, he cannot recover them. The reason why he cannot is that he paid them in pursuance of a contract which is immoral in the eyes of the law and which the court will therefore not enforce. This rule regarding immoral contracts comes from the Common law which puts debts contracted in gambling or by betting into this category. To indulge in gambling or betting is not unlawful, i.e., not punishable as a crime, *but the courts discourage the practice by refusing to compel a debtor to pay what he owes. They apply, as in this case, the Roman maxim to the effect that where the claims of both parties to the suit are equally invalid, the defendant is in the better position in that he can retain what he holds because the law declines to intervene in the matter.*

Eshowe: 13 February 1941. Before E. N. Braatvedt, President; F. H. Ferreira and W. G. Stafford, Members of the Court.

Appeal from Court of Native Commissioner, Mahlabantini.

STAFFORD (Member):

The plaintiff sued the defendant in the Chief's Court for the return of four head of cattle advanced as *lobolo* in respect of an anticipated customary unión between plaintiff and defendant's daughter and obtained a judgment for that number.

The defendant appealed. In the course of plaintiff's evidence, it was disclosed that he had delivered nine head of cattle as *lobolo*, that they increased by two head and that defendant had repaid seven head. During the trial before the Chief, another head had been returned, leaving, therefore, a balance (including the increase, probably still calves) of three head. It further transpired from his evidence that the girl had lived with plaintiff for a while and that a feast had been held and there had been some question raised at the feast as to why an official witness was not present. Plaintiff admitted that he had a wife whom he had previously married by Christian rites and that the reason why the engagement was broken off was that he was told that he could not take a second wife. He admits that he knew that he had no right to take a second wife and that it was against the law.

At this stage of the proceedings defendant's counsel asked for the dismissal of the claim on the ground of the illegal contract and the application was granted.

The plaintiff has appealed, chiefly on the ground that his claim is based not on the illegal contract (as no union had taken place) but simply on the fact that the cattle were *sisa* cattle in terms of Section 85 (1) of the Code. In other words,

115

he wished to avoid the consequences of his participation in an illegal transaction by saying that the cattle are still his and he has the right to recover them from defendant's possession. This is an expediency which has been frequently resorted to by litigants with success.

Our sister-court has, however, already laid down in *James Sogayise* v. *Morgan Mpahleni*, N.A.C. (C. and O.) S.D. No. 9/1931—a case on all fours with this one—that such cattle are not recoverable as the payment of *lobolo* is part of and a preliminary to the union. If this case is followed plaintiff would have no redress.

The application of the maxim *in pari delicto potior conditio defendentis*, regarding the rights of parties under an illegal contract, has been profoundly modified by the recent decision of *Jajbhay* v. *Cassim*, [1939], A.D. 537. This decision now gives a court a discretion to provide relief. In terms of the headnote of the report :

"The Court will not enforce rigidly the general rule '*in pari delicto potior est conditio defendentis*', but will come to the relief of one of the parties where such a course is necessary in order to prevent injustice or to satisfy the requirements of public policy."

The rule itself exists, but the court may in a suitable case, based on the principle enunciated, take the case out of the general rule.

The decision goes further and lays down that the question of recovery must not be made dependent on the test as to whether the plaintiff relies on the contract or not. The position appears to be that the rule may still be applied as long as the party had paid or delivered something in connection with an illegal contract.

Applying the above principle to this case, we find that this is not a case in which the court should use its discretion in coming to the aid of the plaintiff because :—

> (1) In the circumstances disclosed no manifest injustice has been done to the plaintiff and the defendant

has not been unduly enriched at his expense.

(2) The interests of public policy are better served by depriving the real wrongdoer of the residue of the unclaimed *lobolo*.

The appeal is dismissed with costs but the Native Commissioner's judgment is altered to read: "The appeal is allowed with costs and the chief's judgment altered to one for Defendant, with costs."

BRAATVEDT, P.: I concur.

FERREIRA (Member): For the sake of clarity I desire to state that in agreeing that the appeal should be dismissed with costs, I base my decision on the fact that in the case of *Jajbhay* v. *Cassim*, 1939, A.D. 537, the learned Chief Justice laid down that where public policy is not forseeably affected by a grant or refusal of the relief claimed, a court of law may well decide in favour of doing justice between the individuals concerned and so prevent unjust enrichment.

I consider that it is not in the interests of public policy for Natives married by Christian rites to be encouraged to contract so-called customary unions in contravention of the law and I, therefore, hold that the present case is not one which can be considered to be an exception to the maxim *in pari delicto potior conditio defendentis*.

Silwanetshe Cili v. Mbopeni Ntombela, 1941 N.A.C. (Natal and Transvaal) 16.

The property rights in a girl, i.e., the right to receive the lobolo to be paid for her at some future date, can be transferred by her father to another person as security for a debt. But in that event the man paying the lobolo must still pay it to the father, not to the third person because, for one thing, the cattle paid as lobolo may be more than the debt which gave rise to the transfer of the right. Transfer is a form of security indicating how the debt will be paid in due time, i.e., the source from which the debtor will obtain the cattle that he owes.

The Chief no doubt failed to appreciate this distinction. He also acted improperly in ordering the third person, who was not a party to the case, to pay the cattle to the plaintiff.

Eshowe : 12 February 1941. Before E. N. Braatvedt, President ; F. H. Ferreira and W. G. Stafford, Members of the Court.

Appeal from the Court of Native Commissioner, Mtunzini.

BRAATVEDT, P. (delivering the judgment of the Court) :

Appellant sued a man named Mgodi Biyela for six head of cattle.

The Native Chief who heard the case, gave the following judgment :—

"For plaintiff with costs. The plaintiff is entitled to the *lobolo* of defendant's daughter, Sandolo."

Probably what the Chief meant was that the judgment should be satisfied with cattle which Mgodi would receive by way of *lobolo* for his daughter, Sandolo, on her marriage ; but the appellant's contention is that he was awarded the property rights in the girl, which would mean that he was given a judgment for more cattle than he claimed, since the girl's *lobolo* would be eleven head of cattle.

Respondent was engaged to the girl Sandolo at the time. After the Chief had given the judgment he sent for respondent and there is evidence that he instructed him to pay the *lobolo* cattle for Sandolo to the appellant, and not to her father, Mgodi, but the respondent states that he did not agree to do so.

He paid the full *lobolo* to Mgodi. Appellant obtained eight of the *lobolo* cattle through Mgodi, and thereafter sued the respondent in the Court of the Native Commissioner for the balance of three head which he had failed to obtain from Mgodi.

The Native Commissioner gave judgment for the defendant (now respondent), with costs. This appeal is from that judgment.

The Chief had no authority to instruct the respondent to pay the *lobolo* cattle to appellant. Respondent was not a party to the action between appellant and Mgodi. He rightly paid the *lobolo* to the girl's father.

118

The appeal is dismissed with costs, and the judgment of the Native Commissioner is confirmed.

Malewu Thela v. Mabaleni Nkambule, 1940 N.A.C. (Natal and Transvaal) 113

In this case the court disallowed a claim for lobolo on the ground that the total dowry demanded was excessive—this in spite of the fact that there was an agreement between the parties on the amount. The court disapproves of the tendency to commercialise lobolo and marks its disapproval by declining to enforce a contract that provides for too large a dowry. The decision is apparently based partly on considerations of "public policy" and partly on the view (which is arguable) that Native law means original tribal custom, not custom as practised to-day. The court applies to lobolo the Common law view that even an explicit contract may have to be interpreted in the light of general social considerations.

Ermelo : 27 September 1940. Before E. N. Braatvedt, President; W. H. Hare and H. A. van Rooyen, Members of the Court.

Appeal from Court of Native Commissioner, Carolina.

BRAATVEDT, P. (delivering the judgment of the Court):

Respondent's daughter, Dina, married appellant's son, Lotter, in 1938. Appellant made himself responsible for the payment of *lobolo* for the girl. Five head of cattle were paid by him on account at the time of the marriage.

In March, 1940, the respondent sued the appellant for seven head of cattle, or alternatively for £28, their value, alleging that the *lobolo* which had been agreed upon was twelve head of cattle.

When the case came before the Native Commissioner, the defendant (appellant in this court), admitted liability to the extent of two head of cattle only. He contended that the *lobolo* agreed upon was seven head of cattle and not twelve head.

The Native Commissioner at once entered judgment for the plaintiff (respondent in this court) for the two head of cattle, but thereafter recorded evidence led by both parties and

119

entered a further judgment for plaintiff for five head of cattle, or their value, £20, with costs.

From the record it would appear that two judgments have been given in favour of the plaintiff in the lower court in the one case, namely, for two head of cattle, and another for five head of cattle or £20. The Native Commissioner, however, states in his reasons for judgment that he meant that the first judgment should merge in the second and that the final judgment is for five cattle, or £20.

The grounds of appeal are that the Native Commissioner should have accepted the evidence of the defendant (appellant in this court), and that as the girl, Dina, had borne two children to another man before she married Lotter, the *lobolo* payable for her would be considerably less than that for a girl who had not borne children. A further ground of appeal is that the Native Commissioner gave two judgments, but he has elucidated that point in his reasons for judgment.

The Native Commissioner finds as a fact proved that the contract was for twelve head of cattle, but bases his judgment on plaintiff's (respondent's) statement when giving his evidence, that if twelve head had been paid to him, he would have repaid two head.

Plaintiff's evidence is supported by that of his two wives and a man named Mnisi, who states he was present when the parties agreed that twelve head of cattle should be paid, but that he then left and knows nothing further.

Plaintiff and his wives give conflicting evidence in regard to the number of children borne by Dina before her marriage and the number of cattle paid by her first husband or seducer. The Native Commissioner states that he rejected the evidence of defendant and his brother because they gave most conflicting evidence on a very important point. The record does not disclose any discrepancy in their evidence. Defendant does say that he and his brother took Dina back to her father with five head of cattle and his brother says that she preceded them by a few days. That is probably the "conflicting evidence" to which the Native Commissioner refers, but the defendant was not cross-examined on the point, which, in any case, had no bearing on the case. A Native would say that he took a girl back to her father with the cattle even if she preceded him by a few days—that is a Native's way of saying it.

The parties to the action appear to be Swazis judging from their clan names, and the customs of the Swazis and Zulus were at one time very similar, although they may at the present time differ in some respects because Zulu law has been codified whereas there is no written Native law in the Transvaal. It is, I think, an accepted fact that originally there was no fixed *lobolo* amongst the Bantu tribes. With the Zulus the custom was that a bridegroom would pay a few head at the time of the marriage, and would supplement the number after marriage should his father-in-law be in difficulties, but the total number of animals paid rarely exceeded five or six head; in many cases it was less.

The same custom probably obtained in other tribes akin to the Zulus, such as the Swazis. The Natal Code raised the number of cattle payable to ten head. There is reason to believe that outside of Natal, other tribes for which no written law has been provided, have in comparatively recent times, in many cases departed from their ancient customs by demanding and receiving higher *lobolo* than did their forefathers.

Tribal control has slackened and it is only natural that, in the absence of restrictive legislation, advantage should be taken of the opportunity to enrich oneself. When Natives say that the custom in their particular tribe is that a high number of cattle is payable as *lobolo*, such an assertion should be viewed with suspicion as it is probably not of ancient origin.

In Natal to-day, if a girl bears two children before marriage, her *lobolo* would not exceed eight head of cattle, for one beast would be deducted for each child born from the ten head fixed by the law. Before European occupation of the country, the number would have been less than that.

Excessive demands in the Transvaal where there is no written

121

Code, should not be allowed, not only because they have no foundation in original Native law, but also because they tend to prostitute the underlying object and purpose of *lobolo* and to commercialise the transaction. There appears to be no reason why the already high number of *lobolo* cattle fixed by the Natal Code should be exceeded by any tribe living in the Transvaal.

On these grounds the *lobolo* for Dina should not have exceeded eight head of cattle in spite of any agreement to the contrary which might have been made by the parties concerned.

I am not impressed by the evidence of the plaintiff and his witnesses. Dina was at some time or other convicted of cattle stealing and was fined £3. Whether her conviction took place before or after her marriage to Lotter, the record does not say, but her father, the plaintiff in the court below, paid the fine on her behalf and also paid £3 to a lawyer to defend her. He thereafter demanded a refund from the defendant, and when the money was not forthcoming, he instituted the present action.

The Native Commissioner, however, accepts his story that it was agreed that twelve head of cattle should be paid for Dina, and I am not prepared to hold that he arrived at a wrong finding as he had the advantage of seeing the witnesses, but for the reasons stated, this court cannot hold that such an agreement should receive judicial sanction.

The position which has been outlined is that applicable to Natives who are commoners. Chiefs are, of course, entitled to a higher *lobolo*. From the record it appears that the plaintiff is a commoner.

A *lobolo* contract is normally between the bridegroom and the bride's father, but in the present case the defendant (appellant) accepts personal liability.

This court has held that £3 represents a fair value of the average *lobolo* animal in the Transvaal.

The appeal is allowed with costs, and the Native Commissioner's judgment is altered to read: "For plaintiff for three head of cattle, or their value, £9, with costs."

Joseph Mbani v. Regina Mbani, 1939 N.A.C.
(Cape and O.F.S.) 91

The question here was whether a refusal by the husband to pay lobolo in a marriage under the Common law is tantamount to desertion on his part, i.e., is his refusal such conduct as makes the living together of the parties intolerable and so justifies his wife in leaving him? (Desertion does not merely mean a physical leaving of A by B: it may be "constructive desertion", i.e., such conduct by A as justifies B in leaving him. In that case A has deserted B although it is she who leaves him.)

Now it is clear that a marriage between Natives might become intolerable to either party for a reason that would not affect Europeans, e.g., a continual accusation of practising witchcraft. But is a husband's refusal to pay lobolo or more lobolo, such a reason? Admittedly, it makes the wife exceedingly unhappy but if we say it justifies her in leaving him, we are in effect making the payment of lobolo an essential, not merely an optional, element in marriage under the Common law. It is, of course, essential in a customary union but it has hitherto been regarded as optional in a marriage in the sense that it is only enforceable if the husband contracted to pay it.

An alternative view to that taken by the President here is that when a Native woman enters a marriage, she may be deemed to accept certain assumptions, one of which is that payment of lobolo for her is only on a ontractual basis and not inherent in the relationship with her or her guardian. If the opposite assumption is maintained, the parties should enter a customary union, not a marriage.

This case is further complicated by the fact that the husband did apparently pay the first instalment of obolo voluntarily but refused to pay another of the amount asked.

The court held that the plaintiff had not proved his case. The decision is a highly debateable one.

The President quotes Hendrik Brouwer (1625–83) whose treatise "De Jure Connubiorum" was published in 1664. Although the main

*object of the book was to expound the marriage laws of the Nether-
lands, it also deals with marriage among the Hebrews, Romans,
Germans and other European nations, and with the Canon law.
To decide a legal question of marriage between Bantu in the twentieth century, the court may refer to a writer on Roman-Dutch law
in the seventeenth century.*

Kingwilliamstown : 9 August 1939. Before A. G. McLoughlin,
Esq., President, Native Divorce Court.

McLoughlin, P. :

Plaintiff sued defendant for restitution of conjugal rights
failing which for divorce on the ground of malicious desertion.

Defendant admitted leaving plaintiff because he would not
pay his *lobolo*. She was now with her people awaiting adjustment of the matter of *lobolo*.

In his evidence plaintiff stated that his mother was living
with him, the only son, at East London, and his wife was not
on good terms with her.

He originally paid one beast on account of dowry. Defendant's brother came and demanded more dowry. Plaintiff
offered £2 10s. which sum was refused, the amount demanded
being £5, and thereafter Defendant was *teleka*-ed.

Plaintiff made no attempt to meet the demand of defendant's
people for dowry and did not *putuma* her. Instead he went to
the Native Affairs Department, East London, and the summons
instituting this action was issued.

Plaintiff's only other witness was his mother, who corro-
borated his evidence to the effect that defendant's brother came
demanding £5 on account of *lobolo*, refused the £2 10 s.
offered, and thereafter took away the defendant with her
belongings.

Analysis of Brouwer's definition of malicious desertion (*De
Jure Connubiorum.* Lib. 2 Cap. 18 N. 12) followed in *Webber* v.
Webber [1915] A.D. p. 239, makes it clear that the defendant
cannot be regarded as a malicious deserter.

He says "*Malitiosus desertor est, qui nulla justa aut necessaria
causa coactus, ex anima quadam levitate et malitia, vel impatientia*

freni conjugalis, uxoris et liberorum curam abjicit, eos deserit, et oberrat sine animo redeundi."

A malicious deserter is one who, constrained by no just or necessary cause, but owing to a disposition approaching fickleness and ill-will, or through impatience of the marriage tie, casts off the care of wife and children, forsakes them, and wanders about with no intention of returning."

Now it may be contended that non-payment of *lobolo* is not a just cause for detaining a wife under the *teleka* custom, because of the civil or Christian marriage. For by analogy non-payment of *dos* to the bride's parents gave rise to no cause of divorce, for by Civil law, marriage is begun in and rests on consensus not wealth, and is constituted without the dowry. *"Multa minus conceditur divortium XXX vel dos promissa ab uxoris parentibus non solvitur: animum non opibus initur et nititur conjugium, et sine dote consistit."*—Brouwer : De Jure Connub 11 Cap. ult. A. 23.

But the definition of malicious desertion, given by Brouwer in the above extract and repeated by him in the last chapter of his book, dealing with the position obtaining in Holland, emphasises the fact that there is no desertion if one spouse leaves the other for just or necessary cause and not with evil or idle purpose or impatience of the marriage tie, forsaking the other spouse and the family with no intention of returning.

In the present case non-payment of *lobolo* is a matter which goes deeper than the question of wealth. It is a matter directly affecting the dignity of the female spouse. In Native society it would incur odium and there is here rather analogy with the principle involved in such cases as *Duncan* v. *Duncan* [1937], A.D. 310 and *Theron* v. *Theron*, [1924], A.D. 244, where the conduct and the unreasonable attitude of the husband is responsible for making cohabitation *ondragelijk*. It is difficult to convey to a European mind not versed in Native custom the reaction of the wife on this question of *lobolo* or its absence. To the Native the position is perfectly clear and the wife is, in their system, justly detained for non-payment.

This court though basing its practice on that of the Supreme Court, must have regard to Native mentality, if not Native custom, in dealing with the human factor. This aspect was fully discussed in Gama v, Gama, [1937], N.A.C. (T. and N.), page 77.

In the present case the wife has not left her husband, home and family with an evil intent of abandoning them and never returning—she is ready and willing to return as soon as plaintiff makes it possible for her to do so with dignity.

Following the ruling in Gama v. Gama the court absolves the defendant from the instance with costs.

Jackson Sonqishe v. Bransby Sonqishe, 1943 N.A.C. (Cape and O.F.S.) 6

This case illustrates some of the complications that arise from the well-known custom whereby a father allots a daughter, i.e., the lobolo to be received for her, to a particular son. The plaintiff here is an eldest son and heir whose own deceased father, he alleges, was entitled to the lobolo of his aunt. His claim is contested by his uncle, who alleges that the lobolo of his sister (plaintiff's aunt) was allotted to him during his father's lifetime. Whether the allotment was made many years ago is a question of fact that had to be decided in the light of the usual practice followed by Natives on such occasions. The court decided it in favour of the original plaintiff, reversing the decision of the Native Commissioner in the court of first instance.

The reference to Seymour's "Native Law and Custom" (p. 113) reads as follows —"When allotting daughters to different members of his family, it is customary for a father to consult all interested persons. This however is not absolutely necessary, and a father need not consult even the heir to whom the allotted girl would otherwise belong." Seymour cites the case of Nyakata v. Dabula, which was heard in the Appeal Court at Kokstad in 1903.

See also Whitfield's "South African Native Law", pages 45, 46, and 341.

Kokstad : 1 February 1943. Before J. W. Sleigh, Esq., Acting President, Messrs. M. Israel and J. M. Rothman, Members of the Court.

Appeal from the Court of the Native Commissioner, Mount Frere :

SLEIGH (Acting President) delivering the judgment of the court.

The dispute between the parties concerns the dowry of a girl Janet. The facts, which are not disputed, are as follows. The late Philip Sonqhishe had only one wife, Georgina. They had three sons, James, Jackson (defendant) and Gray ; and five daughters, Cecilia, Grace, Mary Ann, Janet and Jocely. Plaintiff is the eldest son of James. Janet was born about 1903. About the year 1923 and after Philip's death, Janet became engaged to one Nabi Nonganga who paid seven cattle as dowry to James. At this time the whole family was still living at Philip's kraal. Janet rejected Nabi who brought an action against James for the return of the seven cattle. The record of this case, which has been put in, shows that judgment was given in favour of James, but both sides now say that the seven cattle were returned to Nabi. Subsequently one Albert Ncapai desired to marry Janet and paid two cattle by word of mouth to plaintiff, but nothing came of this engagement. Defendant says that he was not aware of this engagement. Janet attended the Tsolo Industrial School and the fees were paid by defendant. About 1938 Janet became engaged and married James Mbebe who paid nine cattle and two horses as dowry. At the time she was living at defendant's kraal and was married from the kraal, defendant supplying her with a marriage outfit valued at £38. The marriage took place while defendant was in Johannesburg, and on his return, about 1940, plaintiff demanded the cattle from him. One of the dowry had died and there had been two increase. Defendant refused to hand over the cattle and claimed that Janet had been allotted to him by his late father Philip. The Acting Native Commissioner was not satisfied that the allotment had been made and gave judgment for plaintiff for ten cattle or their value, £50, and two horses or their value, £20, and costs. Defendant now appeals on the merits against this judgment.

The onus of proof is of course on defendant, and it has been repeatedly held in this court that where a party to an action alleges facts which are at variance with normal Native custom, these facts must be proved by strong and convincing evidence. The evidence given by defendant, Janet and Gray is as follows. About 1911 their father Philip called his family together and allotted Grace to James, Janet to defendant and Jocely to Gray. Cecilia was then already married and Mary Ann had eloped. They state that defendant maintained Janet and paid her school fees, and that about 1924 defendant established his own kraal where his wife and Janet then went to live. They state that the people who were present at the allotment were Philip, his wife Georgina, Philip's brother Thomas and his sons James, defendant and Gray, and that the girls Grace, Janet and Jocely were called into the hut where the discussion took place and were informed of the allotments. Of the people who were present Philip, Georgina, Thomas and James are dead. The record does not disclose whether there were other relatives in the Transkei who could have been called to the meeting. Dasayi, who at that time lived in Bolotwa Location in Idutywa District, is presumably the same person as Dasayi Nongana who gave evidence for plaintiff, but he is merely related to Philip by marriage, his father having married Philip's sister. Gray states that James received Jocely's dowry for the reason that he married before her and he requested James to pay his dowry on the understanding that the latter could reimburse himself by taking Jocely's dowry. There is nothing unusual in this. He has no axe to grind, as he is not to-day claiming Jocely's dowry. He works in Johannesburg where he has been since 1927. It is, therefore, improbable that he would give false testimony against plaintiff who must be regarded as the head of the family, unless there is a good motive and there is admittedly none.

The custom of allotting daughters to sons is well established.

It has acquired a two-fold object, namely, to enable the sons to *lobola* for their own wives with the dowry received for the daughters, and to relieve the father of the expense of maintaining and educating the daughters. This being so, the admitted facts that Janet was living at and was married from defendant's kraal, that he paid her school fees and that he provided her marriage outfit, require explanation. Defendant and Janet say that she had been living at his kraal from 1924 to 1938. Plaintiff and his mother Esther deny this, but they contradict themselves. They first say that Janet was married from James' kraal, but later had to admit that this was not so. If Janet had not been allotted to defendant it is unlikely that he would have assumed responsibility for her education without some prior agreement with James for reimbursement of the expenses to be incurred. And, lastly, if defendant had provided the marriage outfit on behalf of plaintiff, he would have disposed of some of the dowry cattle to defray the expenses and would not have paid for it out of his own resources. Plaintiff and his witnesses say that they never heard of the allotments, and that no claim was made when Nabi paid dowry for Janet. Plaintiff's age is not given but if the dowry for his mother was paid out of Grace's dowry, then his mother must have been married after the allotment. Consequently, one does not expect them to be able to give positive evidence that no allotment had been made, but it is significant that not a single member of Philip's family has come forward to support plaintiff's case. He had to rely on Xetywa and Dasayi, the one merely a member of the same clan and the other related only by marriage. Neither of them would have been consulted by Philip in regard to family matters. The evidence of the headman does not carry the case any further.

Plaintiff further points to the fact that James and not defendant was sued by Nabi for the return of the engagement cattle. There is nothing strange in this, since the dowry was paid to James at his kraal and he was in control of the cattle at the time of the action.

It has been urged on behalf of respondent that Philip should have called all his relatives to witness the allotment, and his failure to do so was contrary to Native custom, but it is clear from the authorities cited by Mr. Zietsman, for appellant, that this is not so. The allotment of girls is a family, not a public matter, and only the persons directly affected by the allotment should be present and even this is not absolutely necessary (see Seymour's *Native Law and Custom* at p. 113 ; *Pato* v. *Pato*, 2 N.A.C. 25 ; *John Bomela* v. *Isaac Bomela*, 4 N.A.C. 71, and *Manjingolo* v. *Manjingolo*, 4 N.A.C. 168).

We are satisfied that the allotment was made and defendant is therefore entitled to Janet's dowry.

The appeal is allowed with costs and the judgment of the court below altered to one for defendant with costs.

Andrew Ramncwana v. Goli Siyotula, 1937 N.A.C. (Cape and O.F.S.) 172

In this case plaintiff was married to Regina under the Common law and they had a daughter, Margaret. Twenty years ago they parted, Regina going to live at the kraal of her younger brother, the defendant. When Margaret got married in due course, the dowry cattle paid for her were pledged by Regina to a trader in return for her daughter's wedding outfit. Later plaintiff, Margaret's father, claimed the dowry or part of it, from defendant. An interesting feature is defendant's plea that Regina, plaintiff's wife, had the right, well established under the Common law, to pledge her husband's credit for household necessaries. As an alternative defence, he pleaded that plaintiff himself had not finished paying dowry for Regina (although they were married in 1910 and this case was heard in 1937) and that the balance due could be counter-claimed by him as Regina's brother. Somewhat surprisingly, the court held that the fact that plaintiff and Regina had lived apart for twenty years did not in the circumstances prevent him from claiming the dowry for his daughter. Compare this decision with the later case of Shabangu v. Masilela [1939], *N.A.C.* *(Natal and Transvaal), 86 (quoted in the third essay in this book.)*

Umtata : 12 June 1937. Before H. G. Scott, Esq., President,

and Messrs. W. J. G. Mears and W. F. C. Trollip, Members of the N.A.C.

Appeal from Native Commissioner's Court, Qumbu.

In the court below plaintiff (respondent) sued defendant (appellant) for the delivery of 12 head of cattle or their value, £60, being dowry paid to defendant for plaintiff's daughter Margaret.

Defendant eventually filed an amended plea to the following effect:

1. He admits Margaret's marriage but says that only eleven head of cattle of her dowry are in existence. He says the dowry was paid to plaintiff's wife, Regina, and is registered in her name.

2. He says that Regina, to whom plaintiff was married by Christian rites in 1910, pledged seven head of the dowry cattle to a trader for the wedding outfit of Margaret and that he is not responsible for her actions and that the parties are of good social standing and the wedding outfit purchased is not excessive and are necessaries.

3. That in regard to the balance of four head of cattle admitted to be in existence by defendant, he says that when plaintiff married Regina, he paid 10 head of cattle and one horse as dowry and undertook to pay the balance of six head when his daughter married and he pleads a set-off in respect of these cattle.

4. That Regina was driven away 20 years ago by plaintiff and ever since then defendant has maintained her and her two children and he claims to set off against Margaret's dowry *isondlo* due under Native custom.

5. In the event of his contention in paragraph 2 being disallowed, he prays that any stock which is due in terms of paragraph 3 of her plea, be set off.

The Assistant Native Commissioner entered judgment in favour of plaintiff for nine head of cattle or their value £45 (after making allowance for two head for maintenance and one which died).

Against this judgment an appeal has been noted on the following grounds :

1. (a) That the Assistant Native Commissioner erred in law in holding that defendant was liable in respect of the seven head of cattle pledged by Regina, the lawful wife of plaintiff, to Mr. C. G. Burns. That the said Regina is in law by reason of her status as a spouse by Christian rites entitled to bind her husband for necessaries, as in fact the wedding outfit of plaintiff's daughter, Margaret, was proved in the circumstances to be ; that plaintiff was liable for her said action and cannot now claim to be re-imbursed from the defendant.

(b) Erred in law and fact in respect of the seven head of cattle pledged to Mr. C. G. Burns by the said Regina in that no effort was made, as stated by the Assistant Native Commissioner, by the defendant to deprive the plaintiff of possession, solely with the purpose and whereas in actual fact it was proved that plaintiff knew of the pledging of the said seven head of cattle and took no immediate action to restrain his wife, Regina, or defendant from doing so. That plaintiff's silence and subsequent inactivity was a tacit ratification of his wife's action and he is now estopped from claiming the said seven head from the defendant ; that defendant has not benefited from the pledging of the said stock ; and that the action of plaintiff's wife was one that plaintiff would have had to take if the said Regina had lived with him and he was in charge of the said Margaret's marriage ; that the same applies to the stock slaughtered for the wedding ceremony.

2. That the Assistant Native Commissioner erred in holding that defendant was liable under Native custom for seven head of cattle pledged to Mr. Burns, particularly by reason of plaintiff's action in the circumstances arising from the Christian marriage and generally on the ground that the time has now come to put into effect the policy of Native Administration slowly to mould Native custom to our Common law. The evidence goes to show that the parties are educated Natives who have adopted European habits and mode of living and are ripe .

subjects for the aforesaid avowed policy of our Administration.

3. (a) That the Assistant Native Commissioner erred in fact in holding that there was no balance of dowry due by plaintiff to defendant for his wife, Regina, and that his judgment here-anent for plaintiff was against the weight of evidence and probabilities of the case.

(b) That the Assistant Native Commissioner erred in fact in holding that by awarding defendant the balance of dowry claimed he would be acting contrary to custom as it would have the effect of placing defendant in possession of the woman and the dowry as this custom presupposes ; that the marriage in question has been dissolved and without fault of the husband, which are not facts in the present case.

4. That the Assistant Native Commissioner erred in placing an alternative value of £5 per head on the nine head of cattle found by him to be due.

The Assistant Native Commissioner has found the following facts proved :

1. That plaintiff married Regina by Christian rites about 1910.

2. That some six or seven years later Regina returned to her father's kraal, taking with her her daughter, Margaret, and a son.

3. That defendant, Regina's younger brother, is now head of the kraal at which Regina resides.

4. That Regina and her two children have lived at defendant's kraal for some twenty years.

5. That Margaret has recently married and that 12 head of cattle were paid as dowry.

6. That of these one died and seven were pledged by Regina in respect of Margaret's wedding outfit.

We are in agreement with his findings of facts but we are of opinion that the evidence discloses the additional facts :

1. That the dowry for Margaret was paid at defendant's kraal, and that he is head of the kraal and in control of the stock.

2. That plaintiff was not consulted in regard to the marriage of Margaret or the disposal of the dowry paid for her.

133

3. That the parties are Hlubis and follow Native custom.

The evidence as to the amount of dowry paid by plaintiff for his wife, Regina, is contradictory. Defendant alleges that only 10 head and a horse were paid and that plaintiff specially agreed to pay a further six head when his daughter got married. Plaintiff, on the other hand, says that he paid 14 head and a horse, that the 14 head increased by four before marriage and that according to Hlubi custom the increase count as dowry. He denies that he made a special agreement to pay a further six head, but admits that there was no necessity for a special agreement in view of the fact that according to Hlubi custom dowry is fixed at 20 head of cattle and a horse. He contends that as his wife deserted him no further dowry is payable.

It does not seem to make any difference which of the two stories in regard to dowry is the correct one for in either case there would still be a balance of six head unpaid.

In regard to the statement about the increase this is denied by the defence and we are not satisfied that there was any increase. The question as to whether according to Hlubi custom any increase of dowry cattle before marriage counts also as dowry does not come up for consideration.

Plaintiff's assertion that his wife deserted him is not credible in view of the fact that for 20 years he had made no effort to get her back nor has he taken any steps in regard to her alleged adulteries.

Regina's story that she was driven away is the more probable. His claim in respect of Margaret's dowry would not be affected in any case.

In regard to ground 1 (a) of the appeal, the claim in this case is one for dowry which must be treated under Native law and custom. Defendant is head of the kraal and is the proper person to account for the dowry paid at his kraal in respect of Margaret. He cannot avail himself of the defence that plaintiff's wife had authority under Common law to pledge her husband's credit and incur expense at Burns's shop in respect of a wedding outfit thereby disposing of certain seven dowry cattle. Further, the expression "necessaries" does not in law apply to such transactions as those mentioned, and in any case is not a matter which defendant can raise against the plaintiff.

Ground 1 (b) raises a plea of estoppel. This is one which should have been raised in the court below and cannot be taken for the first time on appeal.

The second ground of appeal falls away as the parties admit that they have not abandoned Native custom and under that custom a person who marries off a girl without the consent of her guardian does so at his own risk and has no claim to re-imbursement of wedding and other expenses.

In regard to the third ground we are of opinion that the Assistant Native Commissioner erred in finding that the fact of plaintiff and his wife having lived apart for 20 years disentitled the defendant from claiming the balance of the dowry due in respect of the marriage of plaintiff to Regina. Plaintiff admitted that six head of cattle were due thereon but claimed set-off of four increase to the dowry before the marriage took place.

As already stated the court is not satisfied that there was such increase. Notwithstanding their protracted separation there is nothing in European or Native law to preclude plaintiff's claiming the return of his wife nor is defendant on the contrary barred by Native custom from claiming the balance of dowry due. The Assistant Native Commissioner rightly found that defendant is entitled to two head of cattle for *isondlo* in respect of the two children, Margaret and her brother.

In so far as the fourth ground of appeal is concerned, this court is of opinion that defendant suffers no prejudice owing to the value of the cattle having been fixed at £5 each as they are still in existence and he can deliver them.

The appeal is accordingly allowed with costs and the judgment of the Assistant Native Commissioner is amended to read :—Judgment for plaintiff for three head of cattle or their value, £15 (that is, 12 head less six due as balance of Regina's dowry, two *isondlo* cattle and one which is dead) with costs of suit.

12

SOME CASES OF INHERITANCE

THESE four cases of inheritance, or succession as lawyers call it, present a notable contrast. The first two are concerned with pure questions of Zulu and Shangaan custom respectively. The court is called on to define the way in which the custom works. Its decision is only slightly and indirectly affected by legislation in the first case and not at all in the second or Shangaan case. Knowledge of Shangaan custom, whether in the form of recorded cases or any other published material, is so meagre that the court resorted to its power to summon leading tribal chiefs to its assistance.

The next two cases are entirely different. They are concerned with the interpretation of statutes which have sought to define Native rights of inheritance in certain circumstances. The materials before the court and the technique it applied to them in reaching a decision are exactly the same as they would be in similar cases concerning Europeans. The problem presented is in essence a problem of the Common law, not of Native law.

It is necessary to recognize that the special courts for Natives are to-day dealing with both types of case. Indeed, the type represented by the third and fourth reports reproduced here is probably commoner than that represented by the first and second cases. Pure questions of Native custom untouched by either direct legislation or by current legal technique are relatively rare in the courts. Litigation by Natives is now carried on within a framework of rules and procedure and in the light of judicial doctrines firmly laid down by the Common law. The old informality and vagueness of decisions based on custom have inevitably disappeared in the modern world of law.

Ntsukana, Silwana, and Ntulindawo Dhlamini v. Muziwokufa Dhlamini, 1939, N.A.C. (Natal and Transvaal) 95

The main question to be decided in this case was three-fold:

   (i) *When a Zulu kraal head dies without having conferred status on his wives, who was his chief wife?*

   (ii) *Does the second wife automatically become head of the ikohlo section?*

   (iii) *If the chief wife has no son, does the son of the third wife become the indhlunkulu heir? Is his claim to that position to be preferred to that of the son of the second wife?*

Cf. The Natal Code of Native Law (reprinted in "African Studies", March 1943), Chapter XII. See also W. G. Stafford's "Native Law in Natal", Chapter XII.

It appears from the case that the practice of dividing the kraal into sections, though common, is not universal among the Zulus.

Durban : 3 August 1939. Before E. N. Braatvedt, President, H. G. W. Arbuthnot and R. P. Campbell, Members of the Court.

Appeal from Court of Native Commissioner, Mahlabatini.

BRAATVEDT, P. :—

The respondent brought an action against the appellants in the Court of the Native Commissioner at Mahlabatini, Zululand, claiming certain movable property—including livestock—in the estate of the late Langalibalele Dhlamini.

The Native Commissioner gave judgment for the plaintiff (present respondent) for cattle and other property which the defendants admitted was in their possession, and belonged to the estate of the late Langalibalele.

The defendants (present appellants) appealed against the Native Commissioner's findings on the following grounds :

1. That the proceedings were entirely irregular in that, the matter in dispute being a dispute or question arising out of the administration or distribution of an estate in accordance with Native law, it fell to be determined by the Native Commissioner

in his administrative capacity only and not in his judicial capacity.

2. That the plaintiff was not the heir to the estate of the late Langalibalele Dhlamini, in that plaintiff's mother was, according to law and custom, the wife of the *ikohlo* house and plaintiff had therefore no right of succession to the said Langalibalele Dhlamini.

3. That the third defendant's mother was, according to law and custom, the wife of the *iqadi* house and she was, according to law and custom, the wife of the general heir of the late Langalibalele Dhlamini.

The appeal came before the then President of the Transvaal and Natal Appeal Court and two Native Commissioners who are not sitting as members of the present court. That court arrived at a unanimous decision on the first ground of appeal, namely that a Native Commissioner can hear and determine disputes in regard to succession to a Native's estate in his judicial capacity. The previous decision of this court to the contrary in the case *Mohulatsi* v. *Phanuel and Another* (1932 N.A.C.), was overruled, and the judgment of the Cape Division of the Native Appeal Court in the case *Moshesh* v. *Mohshes* (1936 N.A.C.—C. and O.) quoted with approval. That point need not, therefore, be considered any further.

In regard to the second and third grounds of appeal, the learned President expressed certain views without, however, pronouncing his final decision. The other members of the court hesitated to subscribe to them without first obtaining further expert evidence on Zulu law and custom.

The case was therefore remitted to the Commissioner to take such further evidence as either party might tender and thereafter to forward such evidence to this court which would then give its decision on the second and third grounds of appeal.

It is now for the court as presently constituted to decide those points.

It is, I think advisable—in order to make the position perfectly clear—to restate the facts of the case.

The late Langalibalele Dhlamini was a commoner residing in the Mahlabatini District of Zululand.

He had ten wives whom he married in the following order :

1. Nomtimba Sibiya, who had no children.
2. Nomvelelo Mpanza who bore respondent, another boy and three girls.
3. Oka-Ndabula, who bore the third appellant and a girl.
4. Kobonina Zwane, who bore two sons.
5. Seyini Ntombela, who bore two boys and two girls.
6. Gece Butelezi, who had no children.
7. Newspaper Butelezi, who bore one girl.
8. Nanzeni Shandu, who had no children.
9. Mpompi Mtshali, who had no children.
10. Silingile Zulu, who bore no children.

The first appellant is the son of the late Gojela Dhlamini who died after summons had been issued. Gojela was cited as first defendant, but on his death, before any evidence had been led, his son's name was substituted for his as first defendant. Both Gojela and second appellant were half-brothers of the late Langalibalele Dhlamini.

On the death of Langalibalele, his brothers Gojela and Silwane, accompanied by four of Langalibalele's sons, two of his cousins, and by the Native Chief, appeared before the Native Commissioner who was acting in his administrative capacity.

They reported Langalibalele's death and gave a list of his widows and children. A diagram of Langalibalele's kraal was prepared and all those present agreed that it was correct. The diagram forms part of the record and shows that Langalibalele's hut was at the top end of the kraal with a hut containing wives Nos. 1 and 9 on its immediate right, looking towards the gate, and another hut with wives Nos. 2 and 7 on its immediate left. Further down on the right-hand side, were the huts of wife No. 5 and wife No. 8, while further down on the left-hand side were the huts of wives Nos. 3, 4, 6 and 10.

The Native Commissioner thereupon declared that the

present respondent was the heir to the late Langalibalele.

Later in the same month, the same parties again appeared before the Native Commissioner in his administrative capacity and Gojela then announced that he had assembled the widows of Langalibalele and conferred status on them, and that he had made a division of the estate property, awarding half to the *indhlunkulu* section and the other half to the *ikohlo* section. Second and third appellants were present when Gojela made the announcement and no objection was raised.

His arrangement was that the second wife (respondent's) was head of the *ikohlo* section and to her were affiliated wives Nos. 5, 6, 9 and 8.

Langalibalele's first wife, Nomtimba, was declared to be the head of the *ikohlo* section and to her were affiliated wives Nos. 3, 4, 7 and 10. The position of the huts in the kraal was obviously not considered at all when allocating status to the wives.

The respondent was working as a policeman at Vryheid at the time and did not attend the meeting at the Native Commissioner's office. Gojela sent him a letter informing him of what had been arranged.

About a year later he instituted action in the Native Commissioner's Court, claiming the cattle and other property which had been taken by third appellant and by Ndulo, eldest son of wife No. 4, under the award made by Gojela. He also cited Gojela and Silwane as co-defendants. He states that he did so as they dealt with the estate property. There is no evidence on the record to the effect that Gojela and Silwane derived any personal benefit from the estate. They were obviously entirely disinterested and acted bona fide throughout in an endeavour to arrive at a settlement which to them appeared an equitable one.

In regard to Ndulo, the case against him was not proceeded with as there was no proper service of summons on him.

The plaintiff in the Native Commissioner's Court (present respondent), alleges that he is the heir to the late Langalibalele, and he sued in that capacity for estate property alleged to have been wrongfully appropriated by his half-brothers.

140

No plea was recorded by the Native Commissioner and the only witness to give evidence was the plaintiff (present respondent).

Counsel for defendant took exception to the summons on the ground that plaintiff had no *locus standi in judicio* to sue. He argued that in view of the Zululand Code of Native Law of 1878, the third appellant was the general heir.

The exception was overruled, and the court held that the respondent was the general heir and had the right to sue.

Counsel for both parties thereupon agreed that certain property, which they enumerated, was in possession of defendants and belonged to the estate of Langalibalele.

Judgment was entered for the plaintiff for the property enumerated.

It is admitted that Langalibalele did not confer status on any of his wives during his lifetime.

The questions which have to be decided are the following:

1. When a kraalhead dies without having conferred status on his wife, who must be regarded as his chief wife?

2. Does the second wife automatically become the head of the *ikohlo* section?

3. If the chief wife has no son, does the son of the third wife become the *indhlunkulu* heir, and is his claim to that position stronger than the claim of the son of the second wife?

The case was re-opened by the Native Commissioner of Mahlabatini as ordered by the Appeal Court. Witnesses holding responsible positions gave evidence on Native law and custom. Other witnesses spoke about the formalities which were observed at Langalibalele's funeral.

It is proved by overwhelming evidence—and indeed admitted by all parties concerned—that Gojela pointed out the grave site, and carried the deceased's weapons at the burial. The respondent and his full younger brother were unavoidably absent, but the third appellant attended the funeral. He took no leading part in the proceedings. It is alleged that he was very ill at the time and unable to stand over the grave.

The fact that it was deceased's brother who conducted the funeral proceedings is, *prima facie*, an indication, according to Native custom, either that the heir was not present, or that there was at that time uncertainty as to who was the heir.

As the third appellant was present, one would have expected him to have pointed out the grave site even if he was ill if he and those present had known that he was the heir.

The evidence given by the so-called expert witnesses on Native law and custom is conflicting. They all agree that when a kraalhead dies without conferring status on his wives, his brothers meet and decide on the position which each widow should occupy. That is undoubtedly the procedure generally adopted throughout Zululand.

The expert witnesses, however, disagree on other points. Nahlakanhlaka Butelezi, who is a man about seventy years old, holding the position of induna and chief's deputy in Vryheid District, states that in a case such as the one mentioned, the brothers of the deceased always appoint the woman first married as the chief wife, and if she has no sons, then the son of the second woman married becomes the heir to the estate, wives ranking according to their order of marriage. He further says that there is never an *ikohlo* or *iqadi* where the kraalhead has died without having arranged his kraal affairs. Nkantini, who is an important Chief in Zululand, holds a different view.

He also states that the first wife of a commoner is always appointed to the position of chief wife. He goes on to say:

"The *ikohlo* is chosen from any of the remaining wives, but it is Native law for brothers to make the second woman the *ikohlo* and the third woman is placed in the *indhlunkulu* (chief house)".

He says that it is not usual for a commoner to declare an *ikohlo* wife and that the position of the huts carries no weight where no declaration has been made and that the second wife is automatically the *ikohlo*. In this view he is supported by Mciteki Zulu, who acted as chief of an important tribe for a lengthy period.

142

The expert witnesses are all Zulus, and they all no doubt spoke from a firm conviction that the Zulu law as expounded by each of them was the correct one.

Since the Zulu War of 1879 there has been no national gathering such as the *umkosi* of the olden days where the laws of the land were proclaimed by the King acting in consultation with his principal chiefs and headmen, and it is therefore only to be expected that diversity of opinion on certain points has arisen in different tribes especially as the present generation has limited opportunities of ascertaining all the intricacies of Native law and custom. It is, therefore, dangerous to place very great reliance on the evidence of so-called Native experts in all cases.

The Native Codes of 1878 and 1891 which were compiled after exhaustive enquiries from the older generation of Natives and from magistrates with wide experience, who were in many cases excellent linguists, are perhaps a safer guide to refer to than is the opinion of present-day Zulus.

It is clear from the Codes of 1878, 1891 and 1932 that the first wife of a commoner is the chief wife.

Under the 1878 Code, which applied to Zululand, until 1927, she was presumed to be the chief wife but it was competent for a kraalhead, although a commoner, to appoint any other woman to the position. Since 1891, that privilege has been taken away in Natal proper, and the 1932 Code which now operates both in Natal and Zululand, has taken away the privilege which the Zululand Natives enjoyed under the 1878 Code. It is now universal law in both sections of the province that the first wife of a commoner is the chief wife.

On the first question for decision, it must be held that Langalibalele's first wife was his chief wife. The law presumed her to be so, and her late husband's brothers cannot now relegate her to an inferior position.

The question of *ikohlo* and *iqadi* is a more complicated one.

The term *iqadi* is better known in Natal than in Zululand, where the word *umnawe* is generally used to denote the *iqadi* heir.

Although Chief Nkantini says that it is not usual for a commoner to declare an *ikohlo* wife, I am of the opinion, based on long experience as a Native Commissioner in Zululand, that it frequently happens that *ikohlo* and *umnawe* houses are nominated, especially by men with many wives, and that the brothers of a deceased husband often make such appointments when he has failed to do so. It is, however, without a doubt, not a practice which is observed by every commoner. There are many kraals where no such appointments are made either during the husband's lifetime or after his death.

It would appear that the custom is not practised to the same extent in Natal proper.

For example in the case Msongelwa v. Mrau (N.H.C. 1907), Chief Silwane, head of the powerful and well-known Cunu tribe, said that there was no such thing as an *ikohlo* in his tribe.

I shall now refer to some of the decisions given by the Natal Native High Court on the question in issue.

The Judges of that court were in several instances men who had wide experience in dealing with Natives; who spoke the Zulu language excellently, and who were well versed in unwritten Zulu law. Some of the cases came from Natal and some from Zululand but the court's rulings were always the same.

In the case Dungumuzi v. Zuya (N.H.C. 1915), Jackson, J. said:

" In the majority of cases the kraals of commoners have only the chief house or *indhlunkulu* to which an affiliation is not infrequently made to ensure the succession or to add to the wealth of that house", and Bennett, J. said:

"In view of the fact that Boyi (the deceased husband) had not created an *ikohlo*, no junior house could be affiliated to the second wife he married".

In the case Sipani v. Mgitshwa (N.H.C. 1904), it was held that the son of a younger house cannot be selected as heir to the chief house before the son of an older house, unless the younger house has been specially and publicly affiliated at the marriage, to the chief house.

144

Campbell, J.P., said:

"The fundamental rule of succession applicable to this case, is primogeniture, namely, the eldest son of the leading house becomes heir at law and the order of nature not to be interfered with unless there has been a special and public affiliation of a younger wife to the chief house of the section of the kraal concerned, for the purpose of providing an heir to it. The order of nature not having been disturbed by affiliation, the fundamental rule of primogenitive succession must be relied on in settling this dispute. No apparent reasons can be traced for Ntemba passing over Mgitshwa and selecting Sipani as his father's general heir. It was a manifestly unjust arrangement and cannot stand the test of equity. The courts should jealously protect the rights of junior heirs, and prevent them from being interfered with by the ignorance and machinations of relatives or the selfish designs of others."

In the case *Laduma* v. *Bhevu* (N.H.C. 1905), it was held that affiliation, to be valid, should be publicly declared on the day of marriage, and that expert evidence is only allowable to describe the tribal customs or local usage, but not with respect to general Native law.

The Native High Court has thus consistently held that the rule of primogenitive succession must be followed in all cases unless the kraalhead or husband has otherwise decreed. Judges have also said more than once that it is unusual for commoners to have *ikohlo* and *iqadi* houses, and Chief Nkantini supports this view when he says it is not usual for a commoner to declare an *ikohlo* wife. I feel unable to subscribe fully to that view in so far as Zululand Natives are concerned, but I agree that there are many kraals which have no *ikohlo*.

If Section 26 of the 1878 Code is interpreted to mean that the second wife married automatically establishes the *ikohlo* house and the third wife also automatically establishes the *iqadi* house unless the kraalhead otherwise specially decrees, then the division of a commoner's kraal into the three sections would be a very common thing, in fact almost universal where

145

a man has two or more wives, and yet the Native High Court and the expert evidence given by Chief Nkantini is to the effect that it is unusual.

Again if that interpretation is given to the section then the son of the third woman, being the *iqadi* cannot inherit *indhlunkulu* property until all sons of junior houses affiliated to the *indhlunkulu* have been excused.

In the case before us, the fourth and fifth wives both have sons and their claim to the *indhlunkulu* property assuming affiliation, would take precedence over the claim of the *iqadi* heir.

Although the brothers of a deceased husband often confer status on the widows, and although their decisions are often accepted and acted upon without protest (in one case which came to my notice, the eldest boy of the family who was a son of the first married woman, made no protest when he was declared to be the *ikohlo*), yet no authority has been given to them by any law to so act, and any son who feels aggrieved at their decision is at liberty to institute action in a court of law.

The courts must then decide the issue strictly according to the law.

The object of establishing an *ikohlo* is to circumvent the strict application of the law of primogeniture whereby all property devolved on the general heir. If then, a man with many wives and rich in cattle should die without having divided his kraal into sections, his brothers might appoint an *ikohlo* and affiliate some of the wives to that house so that the *indhlunkulu* heir should not inherit the whole property.

A husband who does divide his kraal into sections would also, if well-to-do, give some of the kraal cattle to the *ikohlo* house. No doubt the motive behind the appointment made in the case before us was that there should be a fair division of the estate property and Gojela's action was actuated by a sense of fair play.

The respondent, however, has not accepted this arrangement, and relies on his legal rights. As Langalibalele's first and chief wife had no sons, the respondent, by the law of primogeniture, as the son of the second wife, becomes the general heir, for his father did not divide his kraal into sections, and his uncles had no legal right to do so.

The decisions of the Native High Court have laid down that in such cases the Code of 1878 applied, and this is a case where the women were married while that Code was in force in Zululand. I am of the opinion that the decisions referred to were correct, for if Section 26 is construed to mean that the *ikohlo* and *iqadi* are automatically established, then as already pointed out, practically all commoners with several wives would have kraals divided into sections and we know that such is not the case.

The new Code of 1932 has not changed the position. Section 97 of the new Code makes it clear that there are not more than two senior houses in the kraal of a commoner, except in certain cases of men of influence or wealth, and not more than three senior houses in the kraal of a chief. The senior houses are known as the *indhlunkulu, ikohlo* and *iqadi*.

The definition of *indhlunkulu* is "the chief house in a kraal"; *ikohlo* is the left-hand senior house of a kraal which has been divided into sections as described in Section 100; and *iqadi* is the right-hand senior house of a kraal which has been divided into sections as described in Section 100. For purposes of succession it ranks next to the *indhlunkulu* section. Houses may be affiliated to each one of the senior houses.

Section 97 (1) (*a*) also provides that whenever a customary union is contracted by a kraalhead, a house, which is either a senior or an affiliated house, is established for the bride, but Section 97 (3) provides that in the absence of affiliation, the various houses in a kraal are distinct from and independent of each other and each may acquire its own property and property rights. Sub-section (3) either contradicts or modifies sub-section (1) (*a*) which makes it imperative that each house established by a union must be either a senior or affiliated house.

Section 99 (2) states that if no formal pronouncement or

declaration of status is made 'by the kraalhead at the time of the celebration of the union, the second wife ranks next to the chief wife and her house becomes a senior house ranking next to the *indhlunkulu*, houses established by subsequent customary unions becoming affiliated to the *indhlunkulu* or the other senior house, *i.e.* the house of the second wife married.

The meaning of this section seems to be that the second woman to marry becomes—in the absence of public declaration —the *ikohlo*. Yet the definition of *ikohlo* is the left-hand senior house of a kraal which has been divided into sections as described in Section 100, which reads as follows :

"A formal pronouncement or declaration of status at the time of the celebration of a customary union is made in pursuance of the intention of the kraalhead to divide his kraal into sections, of which there may be four, though in actual practice, except in the case of chiefs and others of rank, influence or wealth, there are seldom more than two. These sections are (1) *indhlunkulu*, (2) *ikohlo*, (3) *iqadi*, (4) and an inferior section composed of the houses of poor relatives and strangers."

In view of the definition of *ikohlo*, such a house cannot be established except where there has been a formal pronouncement at the celebration of the union as explained in Section 100.

Section 99 (2) seeks to provide for cases where no pronouncement has been made. Although it appears that it was intended that in such case the second woman married should automatically become the *ikohlo*, since she is referred to as a "senior house", yet she cannot be so regarded because of the definition of *ikohlo* read with Section 100.

Section 111 confirms this view, for there it is provided that upon the death of a kraalhead whose kraal has not been divided into sections as in Section 100 described, the heirship to the kraal and *indhlunkulu* property is determined in accordance with the table set out in Section 110, "save that in such a case, there is no *iqadi* or *ikohlo* and the senior houses rank according to the priority of their establishment with the result that if there be no heir in the *indhlunkulu*, or in any house affiliated thereto, recourse is had to the next senior house and its affiliated houses in the order of their affiliation in Section 99 (22) and 111, for those sections refer to cases where no pronouncement has been made at the celebration of the marriage and where no division of the kraal has been made.

If it was intended that there must be affiliation, whether publicly announced or not, then what is the meaning of Section 97 (3) ? The various sections to which reference has been made are so conflicting and ambiguous that it is not possible to interpret the exact intention of the Legislature.

Under the new Code also I can find no authority for departing from the well-established decisions of the courts that the law of primogeniture must be observed where a husband has not divided his kraal into sections.

The general heir is entitled to both the kraal and *indhlunkulu* property, the other sons by junior wives being entitled only to the house property of their respective houses and to such kraal property which may have been given by their father in his lifetime.

As Gojela and Silwane merely endeavoured to make what they considered to be an equitable division of the kraal property and as it was not compulsory for anyone to have accepted their ruling, hey should not in my opinion have been cited as co-defendants in this action, and it is unfortunate that Gojela's minor heir, who had nothing whatsoever to do with the arrangements, should have been brought into court.

In so far as the third appellant, Ntulindawo, is concerned, the Native Commissioner's judgment for kraal property in his possession is correct.

The third appellant must bear all the costs in this matter since he has wrongly contended that he is the general heir.

The order of this court is that the appeal in so far as the third appel ant is concerned is dismissed with costs, but in regard to first and second appellants the appeal is upheld with costs and the Native Commissioner's judgment in their case altered to read: "For the first and second defendants with costs".

Joseph Maganu v. Jim Maganu, 1938, N.A.C.
(Natal and Transvaal) 14

*The precise nature of Shangaan custom relating to marriage, inherit-
ance, and dowry is discussed in this case. The chiefs who were
summoned to act as assessors told the court that the Shangaans do
not divide their kraal as the Zulus and the Xhosa usually do. They
have only one principal house to which all the others are subordinate,
ranking in order of marriage.*

*The numerous questions put to and the replies received from the
Native assessors are appended to the court's judgment in the law
reports.*

Pretoria: 20 September 1937. Before A. G. McLoughlin,
President, P. A. Linington and W. G. Thompson, Members
of the Court.

Appeal from the Court of Native Commissioner, Sibasa.

Judgment reserved and delivered at Durban on 5 February
1938.

McLOUGHLIN, P. :

In the Native Commissioner's Court Joseph Maganu sued
his half-brother, Jim Maganu, for certain 77 head of cattle
received in or about 1916 by defendant's father in respect of
the *lobolo* of plaintiff's full sister Nellie, of which defendant
took possession in 1933.

He also claimed a sum of £40, being cash received by his
father for *lobolo* of plaintiff's full sister, Tsatsawane about 1923,
of which defendant took possession about 1925. Judgment was
entered for defendant with costs.

The evidence discloses that parties are sons of Makandale
Maganu, who lived and died in Masia's Location in the Sibasa
district; that Makandale Maganu was a Shangaan, but it has
not been ascertained to which clan or section of that tribe he
belonged.

The parties removed from the ancestral home, plaintiff about
three years ago and defendant some seven years ago, and are
now residing in different locations—the defendant under Chief

Mhinga of the vaPonga branch of the Shangaans, and plaintiff under Chief Hasane of the same branch.

The case was heard and decided under Shangaan custom. In view of the divergent account; of custom given by the parties and the absence of decisions on the point, this court called to its assistance the leading chiefs of the Shangaan nation as assessors.

From their replies it appears that two systems of inheritance and succession are practised by the Shangaan.

One portion, consisting of the Zuluised element under Chiefs Tulelamahashe and Muhlaba, follow a modified form of Zulu custom in establishing junior houses with the Zulu form of succession and inheritance in those houses.

The other section, including the people of Chiefs Mhinga, Mamitwa and Shikundu, follow a system differing completely therefrom. The eldest son of the first and great wife is universal heir to all the property in all the houses set up by the father. He is burdened with the duty of providing for those houses and especially the *lobolo* of their sons.

It appears, moreover, that under this system all the *lobolo* of daughters of the junior houses accrue to the universal heir; that the custom of *Etula* is not followed; that it is permissible for a father to allocate the *lobolo* of a particular daughter for the use of a son and also to allot to him any other cattle as his own for the purpose mainly of acquiring a wife. Such allocation relieved the father and likewise his heir from further liability to provide a wife for such son.

It would seem, however, that following the decision in *Tafeni* v. *Booi* (3 N.A.C., Transkei, p. 162), *M. Masheme* v. *Scott Nelani* (4 N.A.C., Transkei, p. 43), and *Cebe* v. *Silimela* (6 N.A.C., Transkei, p. 14), the case should be heard under Venda law, for the dispute is in regard to an inheritance which accrued at the death of the father who lived and died in a Venda location. Under Venda custom undistributed property not yet applied to the use of any of the deceased's houses accrues to the universal heir in trust. It would seem that the parties have this

151

idea in mind in contesting the present case for the plaintiff's claim is based directly on an alleged appropriation by the father and the defence is that though the cattle are held in trust for the use of the house from which they were derived, yet having fulfilled the obligation of providing a wife for plaintiff, the latter has no personal claim to the cattle or money.

Neither party relies on the Zulu custom of the accrual of *lobolo* to the bride's house as house property.

It thus appears that the case must be decided on the claim based on a direct appropriation of the *lobolo* of Nellie to plaintiff and that of Tsatsawane to Freddie, the younger brother of plaintiff in the same house. Indeed, plaintiff states (page 3 of typed copy): "It is the custom that an elder son inherits all the father's estate, but these things were given to me by my father to buy a wife."

Dealing first with the claim for the 77 head of cattle derived from Nellie's *lobolo*, the evidence for plaintiff is contradictory, unconvincing and inadequate to establish his contention that an allotment was made to him of Nellie's *lobolo*.

He himself states, "I was not present, but I was told that the *lobolo* to be paid for Nellie was to be mine" . . . "It was to supply me with a wife" . . . "Nellie's *lobolo* was to enable me to get a wife. I did not get the wife." He then proceeds to testify that a woman Ngwabanazela was his wife (now deceased); and that he got her with his own money. "I paid for her myself", he states. He continues "My late father paid the *lobolo* for my wife Ngwamazebandlela. I now say my father did not pay *lobolo* for my wife." He alleges that he was told by Nellie and Mpumla of the allocation—he being then too small himself.

Nellie, who was called by plaintiff, states that her father allocated the cattle to plaintiff—"they were to buy a wife for plaintiff". Then she adds "the *lobolo* for Ngwamazebandlela was paid with a little money when our father was alive. I can't say how much. This money was paid by our father". "All I know about Ngwamazebandlela is that old Maganu paid some (cattle) for her as *lobolo* as a wife for plaintiff."

Plaintiff's only other witness is Mapumule who avers that old Maganu brought six head of cattle to him saying they were the property of Joseph and were a wife for him.

The plaintiff's case is inherently defective. If, as he contends, the cattle were to provide a wife for him, his claim was extinguished when a wife was so provided as Nellie alleges. If the wife was not provided by the old man, Maganu, some explanation for this failure is due. The cattle were there and available. Plaintiff's age was no obstacle under Shangaan custom. In any event he was registered for taxes soon after his father's death.

The record is silent on the point of the winding up of the deceased's estate after the termination of the mourning for the late Maganu when claims of this nature are discussed and settled.

Moreover, the plaintiff, though battling to provide a *lobolo* from his own earnings from 1927 till 1930, apparently never pursued his claim to the cattle provided for this very purpose, if his story be true. He stated, on being recalled by the Native Commissioner, that he first went to defendant to claim his property in 1933. He states : "He (defendant) said the cattle were his. I did not press him for his reasons". He admits he did not go to the Native Commissioner's office to complain.

Apart from the failure to prove that the alleged allotment was made in Council according to custom, the facts and the probabilities are entirely against the plaintiff's contention and he must fail. It is true that defendant has not satisfactorily explained his own delay in assuming control of the cattle in question. He has, however, been in possession since 1933, *i.e.* some 8 years after the death of Maganu. He obtained them from the custodian Mapumule without the use of force and indeed rewarded Mapumule for his services. The handing over of this stock and acceptance of a reward is in Native custom an acknowledgment of the right of the payer to the property in question.

Mapumule's inactivity in resisting defendant's demand, Nellie's remark that since her father's death she has not discussed the matter of the cattle with defendant and plaintiff's own admission that although he complained to his Uncle Breakfast the latter took no action, all go to confirm the impression that defendant was the real owner. It is significant that Breakfast has not been called by plaintiff.

The defendant is therefore entitled to the judgment in his favour although it would appear from defendant's remark "I know these cattle belong to the house of plaintiff. It is true that cattle obtained by a house is for the use of a house", that he is prepared to admit a certain right of plaintiff's house in the cattle.

The true interpretation of these words seems to be found in the replies of the assessors, that while a house continues to stand after the death of the husband cattle placed there remain for the use of that house although ownership vests in the general heir who is charged with the duty of providing a wife for each son of that house and for the upkeep of the house and the maintenance of its inmates.

It will be remembered that the general heir is trustee of the family and holds the property as such under Native custom and not as a sole unencumbered owner as in Common law and it becomes clear that unless there has been a personal appropriation of specific cattle to an individual member of a family a personal claim cannot in Shangaan law or Venda law, whichever be applicable to the parties, be preferred by a younger or junior male of the family to the estate or a portion thereof.

The judgment of the Native Commissioner will therefore not be disturbed in so far as it deals with this item of plaintiff's claim.

Much of the foregoing remarks apply with equal force to the second claim for £40—as between the parties.

This claim, however, is one on which the plaintiff cannot succeed on his own showing. The allotment, if any, is alleged to have been made to Freddie who is the proper person to pursue a claim based on an allotment to him.

Plaintiff's contention to the contrary notwithstanding, the

154

individual responsible for the provision of *lobolo* for Freddie's first wife is the defendant as general heir.

The appeal will accordingly be dismissed with costs.

LININGTON (Member):

Appellant (plaintiff in the court below) had claimed from respondent (defendant) delivery of 77 head of cattle, being six beasts and their progeny received as dowry for his (plaintiff's) sister Nellie, and the sum of £40 received for his sister Tsatsawane.

Defendant in his plea admitted that £60 cash was received by his late father as dowry for Nellie, and £57 cash and two beasts for Tsatsawane but stated that he inherited these sums and cattle. Defendant denied that plaintiff had any claim to the property, according to Native custom.

The law applied in the hearing of the case was Shangaan custom, and judgment was given for defendant with costs.

Plaintiff had appealed against the judgment on the following grounds:

(*a*) That the judgment is against the evidence and against the weight of evidence.

(*b*) That the Commissioner was influenced wrongly in arriving at his decision by a supposed Shangaan custom relating to rights and liabilities arising upon the death of the head of the house.

(*c*) That the Commissioner has not decided correctly whether the contract in regard to the cattle and moneys claimed was in fact entered into by the deceased or not.

(*d*) That the onus which rested upon the defendant at the close of the plaintiff's case has not been discharged by the defendant.

Appellant is a son of the minor house and respondent is the eldest son of the principal house of the late Maganu, a Tshangaan resident in the Sibasa District. Appellant and Nellie and Tsatsawane are children of one and the same house.

Appellant's evidence that his late father said he should have Nellie's *lobolo* is hearsay. He claims that the *lobolo* was to be

155

used by him to acquire a wife and it has not been so used. He states that he married Ngwabanazela (now dead) with *lobolo* earned by his own labour and that "according to our custom my father has to bring me one wife only. If my father dies, then my elder brother has to supply me with a wife. This is a debt assumed by an elder brother when he inherits an estate if the father has not already given the younger son a wife." Appellant after saying that he got Ngwabanazela with his own money, went on to state: "My late father paid the *lobolo* for my wife Ngwabanazela. I now say that my father did not pay *lobolo* for my wife." Nellie giving evidence on behalf of appellant says "All I know about Ngwabanazela is that old Maganu paid some for her as *lobolo* as a wife for plaintiff." She also says that her father died about 1925, that appellant was not of a marriageable age at that time and that Ngwabanazela was not living with him before old Maganu died. Respondent says that he paid the *lobolo* for Ngwabanazela out of property he inherited from his father. Two witnesses testify to the payment of the *lobolo* by defendant.

The court sees no good reason for disturbing the acceptance by the Additional Native Commissioner of respondent's evidence in regard to the source of the *lobolo* for Ngwabanazela based as it is on credibility. Defendant must be held to have discharged the liability upon himself and his father's estate in respect of the provision of a wife for appellant.

Appellant claims that there was a definite allocation of Nellie's *lobolo* to his house and that he is entitled to it and its natural increase. He has no personal knowledge of his late father's action or intention in regard to the *lobolo*. His witness Mapumule says, "I had cattle belonging to old Maganu. He brought them to me saying that they are the property of Joseph. They were six. They were for a wife for him." Nellie says "£60 was paid as my *lobolo*. My father bought cattle with this money. They were six. They were taken to Mapumule's. They were to buy a wife for plaintiff. I was told this by my father." It is clear from the evidence of respondent and the opinions of the Native assessors summoned to the assistance of this court that a kraal head may allocate cattle to the son of minor house but that this must be done with the presence of the members of the family including or with the knowledge of the son of the principal house. A secret agreement of that nature between a father and his minor son is contrary to custom and after the father's death would not be honoured by the other members through lack of proof. Appellant has not shown that this custom was not followed in regard to the alleged allotment of Nellie's *lobolo* to him and respondent denies that a family council was held or that he was informed by his late father of such an allotment. Appellant must be held to have failed on this point.

In regard to appellant's claim for the *lobolo* paid for his sister Tsatsawane, appellant admits that he was very young at the time of the alleged transaction and that he was told "these things" by Shimange who is now dead. He says he saw £57 being paid to his father for Tsatsawane and £40 of this £57 being handed over to Shimange for a wife for his (appellant's) younger brother Freddie Mahasane of the same house, and that respondent was not present. He states that according to custom he and not respondent has to provide a wife for Freddie. He produced one witness (his sister Nellie) who testified that when her father died there was a party at which Shimange produced £40 saying he was told by the old man that this was money for a wife for appellant.

Respondent admits that he received £252 from Shimange being money placed in his charge by old Maganu and that the *lobolo* for Tsatsawane may have been portion of it. He says the *lobolo* was £57 and two beasts, and that it is his duty to provide a wife for Freddie. He says he received the whole of his late father's estate. He denies the statement by Nellie.

Here again there is no evidence that custom was followed in regard to the alleged allotment of Tsatsawane's *lobolo* to applicant. The very slender evidence by appellant and his sister is

157

insufficient proof of the supposed private arrangement between the deceased Maganu and Shimange.

Native assessors Mhinga and Shikundu state that it is the duty of the kraal head to provide *lobolo* for the younger son of a minor house; that if the kraal head is dead that duty falls upon the eldest son of the principal house and that it is not an obligation upon the eldest son of the minor house to supply the *lobolo* of his younger brother. This opinion supports the respondent's views. The same two assessors state that the *lobolo* does not belong to the hut of the girl's mother. On the death of the kraal head the cattle are kept in the same kraal under the heir to the principal house, who is the owner of all the deceased's estate; the huts merely have the use of the cattle that attach to them and they cannot be disposed of except under the authority of the heir of the principal house.

It appears to the court that the above-mentioned assessors described Shangaan law proper and that the customs enumerated by the other three assessors differed because they had in the past been influenced by the Zulu practice. The parties belong to the pure Shangaan race and the court has therefore followed the Native custom applicable to them.

Appellant is not entitled to the dowries of his sisters Nellie and Tsatsawane which respondent lawfully inherited as heir to all the property of his late father.

THOMPSON (Member):

In this matter, which is an appeal from a decision of the Additional Native Commissioner, Sibasa, I concur in the finding of the learned President in whose judgment the facts in this case have been fully set out and do not call for further review.

The parties are the sons of the late Makandale Maganu, appellant being the son of a junior house and respondent the eldest son of the first or great house.

Since the death of their father they have taken up residence in different locations and appellant has sought to recover certain 77 head of cattle taken by respondent which he alleges were allotted to him by his father to obtain a wife; and a sum of

£40 said to have been handed by his father to Shimange with the intention of providing a wife for his younger brother Freddie.

The evidence discloses that the appellant subsequently obtained a wife which he says he got with his own money but according to the evidence of his witness, Nellie, through whom most of his information was obtained, the dowry for this wife was paid by his father probably partly in money and partly with cattle thus relieving the father of any further obligation in respect of *lobolo*.

The parties are both Shangaans and appear to belong to the same section of the Shangaan tribe.

From plaintiff's own evidence and the answers given by certain of the chiefs who were called to the assistance of the court, it is clear that under the rules of succession followed by this section of the Shangaan race, ownership rights in the property of a deceased husband pass to the eldest son of the first house and that other houses have merely a right to the use of property placed in such houses. It therefore follows that whatever rights appellant's house may have to the use of the property he has no personal right to the cattle or the money claimed.

The appellant was evidently aware of the position for he stated in evidence, "It is custom that an elder son inherits all the father's estate." He goes on to say, "but these things were given to me by my father to buy a wife," thus indicating that his claim is based on a right of ownership derived from the alleged allotment of the cattle to him by his father. The allotment, if any, was not however made according to custom and his claim on the evidence adduced must fail.

In regard to the claim of £40, apart from the fact that the alleged allotment of this amount was made in favour of Freddie, appellant stated under cross-examination in the lower court "If my father dies then my elder brother has to supply me with a wife. This is a debt assumed by an elder brother when he inherits an estate if the father has not already given the younger son a wife."

There is no doubt, in my opinion, that he was referring to the general heir and that the dowry for Freddie's first wife must be provided by respondent in his capacity as heir to the estate.

It is true that appellant stated under re-examination "I have to provide Freddie with a wife with this £40," but as this is contrary to custom his claim cannot be upheld.

The appeal must therefore be dismissed with costs.

Piet Malatje v. Estate Late Izak Malatje, 1939, N.A.C. (Natal and Transvaal) 149

This is a case where a Native did what many do—he married both under the Common law and by Native custom. The Native Administration Act of 1927 to some extent protected the rights of a woman, who is a partner to a customary union, and her children when her husband leaves her in order to contract a marriage under the Common law. The Act did not, however, contemplate a case like this one in which the customary union is entered into not before the marriage but after its dissolution through the death of the first wife. The question arose here whether the children of such a subsequent union have any rights of inheritance or whether the whole of the deceased's estate should go to the children of his first marriage. The court, bound by the statute, held that the latter rule must be followed. The result is unsatisfactory and the law requires amendment by further legislation.

Pretoria : 13 December 1939. Before E. N. Braatvedt, President, A. Eyles and T. W. H. D. Ramsay, Members of the Court.

Appeal from the Court of Native Commissioner, Pietersburg.

EYLES (Member), delivering the judgment of the court :

The appeal comes before the court in terms of the provisions of Section 3 (5) of the Regulations under Government Notice No. 1664 of 1929.

The late Isaac Katlatje was married by civil rites on 26 August 1908, to Diana Modibe. About 1917, Diana Modibe died leaving three children, the issue of this marriage, who are still living.

In 1924 Isaac entered into a customary union with one Dina, who has had five children by Isaac, all of whom are still alive. Shortly after this union, Isaac entered into a second customary union with one Helena Matlatje and the issue of this union is four children who are also all still living. Isaac died about March 1936, leaving no will.

At the time of the death of Isaac's first wife, there were apparently no assets in the estate and there is no record of any winding up of the estate at that stage (if such were necessary).

During the subsistence of the customary unions, an estate was amassed—including the purchase of land in about 1933. On the death of Isaac, the question arose as to who should succeed to his estate.

On the 20 May 1936, and acting under the provisions of Government Notice No. 1664 of 1929, the Native Commissioner of Pietersburg district (in which the late Isaac resided), appointed Mr. J. F. Kirsten to administer the estate of the deceased.

On the 20 February, 1939, Mr. Kirsten lodged with the Native Commissioner at Pietersburg his first liquidation account of this estate in which he proposed to hand over the whole of the nett proceeds of the estate in equal shares to the three children of the deceased by his first wife, Diana Modibe, to the entire exclusion of the children by the subsequent customary unions.

To this account objection was taken by Mr. L. B. Gillett on behalf of Piet Matlatje, eldest son of the deceased by his first customary union and it was then submitted that Piet Matlatje should succeed under Native custom to the whole estate to the exclusion of all other children of the late Isaac.

This objection was dealt with by the Native Commissioner in terms of Section 3 (4) of the Regulations mentioned and the Commissioner upheld the allocation suggested by the administrator in the account drawn up by him. It is this decision which is brought in appeal to this court.

Although in the notice of appeal it is claimed that Piet

Matlatje is the rightful and sole heir to the whole of estate of Isaac, this contention was not adhered to when the matter was argued before this court. Mr. Kraut, on behalf of the appellant, stated that he was not prepared to support this view and submitted that the correct view was all twelve children of the late Isaac should share equally in the proceeds of the estate for the reason that the two subsequent customary unions were valid unions, the children of which were legitimate and to whom rights of inheritance had accrued equally with the children of the civil marriage.

Alternatively, he submitted that the estate should be divided into twelve equal parts, three-twelfths to be allocated to the children of the civil marriage for distribution *ab intestato* and nine-twelfths to be allocated to the remaining children *according to Native custom.*

In determining this question it is essential to ascertain what statutory provisions are applicable.

Section 23 (10) (*a*) of Act No. 38 of 1927, empowers the Governor-General to make regulations "prescribing the manner in which the estates of deceased Natives shall be administered and distributed". These regulations were duly published under Government Notice No. 1664 dated the 21 September 1929.

The relevant portion of these regulations is Section 2 (*b*), which reads:

"If a Native dies leaving no valid will, so much of his property as does not fall within the provision of sub-section (1) or sub-section (2) of Section 23 of the Act, shall be distributed in the manner following, viz.:

(*b*) If the deceased had during his lifetime contracted a marriage in community of property or under antenuptial contract, the property shall devolve *as if he had been a European.*"

Section 23 (1) of the Act read as follows:

"All movable property belonging to a Native and allotted by him or accruing under Native law or custom to any woman with whom he lived in a customary union or to any house, shall upon his death devolve and be administered under Native law and custom."

It is not contended that any portion of this estate falls under this head.

(Sub-section (2) of this section does not concern this case.)

The provisions of Section 22 (7) of the Act safeguard the interests of wife and children of a customary union entered *prior* to a civil marriage, but we are here concerned with the rights flowing from customary unions entered into *after* a civil marriage had been dissolved by the death of the wife.

Sub-section (8) of Section 22 reads

"*Nothing in this section or in Section* 23 shall affect any legal right which has accrued or may accrue as the result of a marriage in community of property contracted before the commencement of this Act."

The first marriage of Isaac was such a marriage.

What are the rights, therefore, which accrued to the children of the deceased by his civil marriage? Obviously to succeed *ab intestato* to the estate of their father on his death.

It is argued on behalf of the appellant that, had Isaac married again under civil law, the issue of such second marriage would share equally with the children of the first marriage. That is a proposition which must, of course, be accepted. Such marriage would have been a "marriage in community of property contracted before the commencement of this Act". It was further contended, however, that the customary unions being valid, the children of such customary unions were legitimate and that they should be given a status with the children of the civil marriage for the purpose of succession.

This latter view is one which the court finds itself unable to uphold in view of the express provisions of Section 22 (8), referred to above.

An important and obvious distinction must be drawn between (*a*) the children of a customary union entered into *prior* to a civil marriage whose rights accrue before a civil marriage has been contracted and which are safeguarded by

163

Section 22 (7) ; (b) the children of a civil marriage whose rights are safeguarded by the provisions of Section 22 (8), and (c), the children of a customary union entered into *after* a civil marriage. In the latter case, whatever the status of these children may be in other respects, it is clear that they cannot affect the rights of *succession* which have accrued or accrue to the children of a *prior* civil marriage.

In the absence of any *statutory* rights of succession granted to the third group mentioned above, the further question arises as to whether this court should intervene in the interests of these children. The only answer to this question is that where the legislation has made no provision for succession, it is the duty of this court to enforce those provisions in accordance with the clear directions of the statute.

The conclusion come to, therefore, is that the appeal must fail and the decision of the Native Commissioner is upheld with costs.

Julia Shata v. Mocholo Dugmore Shata, 1942, N.A.C. (Cape and O.F.S.) 42

The deceased here was also married twice, on both occasions under the Common law. By his first wife he had a son Mocholo, the defendant. After her death, he married Julia, the plaintiff. On his death in 1940, Julia claimed to be the sole heir of his property. The court upheld her claim. The regulations regarding succession to property lay down that where a man was married in community of property or by ante-nuptial contract, his estate shall devolve according to the law affecting Europeans. Under the Succession Act of 1934 (which thus also affects Natives), where an estate is worth less than £600, the surviving spouse inherits the whole of it. That is why the deceased's son does not get a share of it in this case.

Kokstad, 20 May 1942 : Before H. G. Scott, Esq., Acting President, Messrs. E. W. Thomas and J. P. Cowan, Members of the Court.

Appeal from the Court of the Native Commissioner, Matatiele.

Scott (Acting President) delivering the judgment of the court.

The facts in this case are as follows :

1. Daniel Shata married one Sylvian by Christian rites on 3 April 1905, in community of property, and Mocholo Dugmore Shata is the eldest son of that union.

2. On 26 August 1919, after the death of his first wife, Daniel Shata married one Julia, community of property being excluded by virtue of Section 5 (1) of Proclamation No. 142 of 1910.

3. Daniel Shata died intestate on 26 December 1940, without having made any allotment of his property to his wife.

4. Mocholo Dugmore Shata was appointed to represent the estate on 31 March 1941, in terms of Government Notice No. 1664 of 1929.

5. Julia Shata, claiming to be sole heiress *ab intestato* of Daniel Shata, applied in the Court of the Native Commissioner at Matatiele for an interdict against Mocholo Dugmore Shata restraining him from alienating any of the assets of the estate pending the institution of an action by her calling upon him for an account of his administration of the estate and delivery to her of the assets.

6. The estate does not exceed £600 in value.

7. A rule *nisi* was granted on the 10 October 1941, returnable on 13 November 1941, the rule to act as a temporary interdict.

On the return day the interdict was discharged and applicant ordered to pay costs, and the appeal is against that order on the ground that appellant is the sole heiress of the late Daniel Shata and as such entitled to the interdict applied for.

Before this court, Mr. Zietsman, for appellant, in the course of his able argument, raised many points of considerable interest and importance ; among others, the consequences in regard to succession to Native estates following on amendments to the law from 1910 onwards and the question as to whether Section 2 (*e*) of Government Notice No. 1664 of 1929 is not

165

ultra vires the powers of the Governor-General under sub-
section (10) of section *twenty-three* of Act No. 38 of
1927. In the view taken by this court of this case it is not
necessary to give any decision on these points raised by Mr.
Zietsman.

It is quite clear that the property in this estate does not fall
within the purview of sub-section (1) and (2) of section *twenty-
three* of Act No. 38 of 1927, and consequently was capable of
being devised by will in terms of sub-section (3) of the same
section. The late Daniel Shata having died intestate his movable
property must be dealt with in terms of Section 2 of Government Notice No. 1664 of 1929. The portions of that Government Notice relevant to this case are paragraphs (c) and (e),
which read respectively as follows:

"(c) If the deceased had during his lifetime contracted a
marriage in community of property or under ante-nuptial contract, the property shall devolve as if he had been a European."

"(e) If the deceased does not fall under any of the classes
described in paragraphs (a), (b), (c) and (d) the property shall
be distributed according to Native law and custom."

The Assistant Native Commissioner held that, as the marriage between the late Daniel Shata and appellant was, in terms
of Section 5 (1) of Proclamation No. 142 of 1910, out of
community of property, it obviously is not one of the forms
of marriage referred to in Section 2 (c) of Government Notice
No. 1664 of 1929 and, therefore, the estate falls to be administered under Section 2 (e) of the said Government Notice.

It is obvious that the decision of this case depends upon the
interpretation to be placed upon Section 2 (c) above quoted.

It was contended by Mr. Elliot, for respondent, that the
court should read into Section 2 (c) between the word "property" and "shall devolve" the words "of the parties to such
marriage".

With this contention this court cannot agree. It is an elementary rule of interpretation that effect must be given to the
ordinary grammatical meaning of the words used.

As Maxwell says in his work on the Interpretation of Statutes (7th Edition, page 3):

"When the language is not only plain but admits of but one meaning, the task of interpretation can hardly be said to arise. . . . . Such language best declared, without more, the intention of the law given and is decisive of it. The Legislature must be intended to mean what it has plainly expressed, and consequently there is no room for construction. It matters not in such a case what the consequence may be.

"Where by the use of clear and unequivocal language capable of only one meaning, anything is enacted by the Legislature, it must be enforced, even though it be absurd or mischievous. The underlying principle is that the meaning and intention of a statute must be collected from the plain and unambiguous expressions used therein rather than from any notions which may be entertained by the court as to what is just and expedient. If the words go beyond what was probably the intention, effect must nevertheless be given to them. They cannot be construed, contrary to their meaning, as embracing or excluding cases merely because no good reason appears why they should be excluded or embraced. However unjust, arbitrary or inconvenient the meaning conveyed may be, it must receive its full effect. When once the meaning is plain, it is not the province of a court to scan its wisdom or its policy. Its duty is not to make the law reasonable, but to expound it as it stands according to the real sense of the words."

In the cases of *ex parte* the Minister of Justice *in re Rex* v. *Jacobson and Levy* (1931, A.D. 466) and *Smith* v. *Clark* (1935, A.D. 224), it was pointed out that it is not for the court to speculate what Parliament might have intended to mean in cases where the words are clear and unambiguous, however surprising the result. Indeed in these two cases the results *were* most surprising, but the court refused to put any other than the natural grammatical interpretation on the words used and refused to add to or take away anything though it seemed obvious that Parliament intended something very different.

167

When the language of a statute, in its ordinary meaning and grammatical construction, leads to a manifest contradiction of the apparent purpose of the enactment, or to some inconvenience or absurdity, hardship or injustice, presumably not intended, a construction may be put upon it which modifies the meaning of the words, and even the structure of the sentence, by, amongst other things, interpolating other words, under the influence, no doubt, of an irresistible conviction that the Legislature could not possibly have intended what its words signify, and that the modifications thus made are mere corrections of careless language and really give the true meaning (see Maxwell at page 198). A sense of the possible injustice of an interpretation ought not to induce judges to do violence to well-settled rules of construction, but it may properly lead to the selection of one rather than the other of two reasonable interpretations (*ibid.* page 174).

Now before the court can modify the language of an enactment it must be satisfied from an examination of the general scope and object of the Act that the words used do not express the real intention of the Legislature and then only when they are capable of two meanings. One of the objects of Act 38 of 1927 was to deal with the administration and distribution of Native estates. Section 23 (3) of the Act as originally enacted provided that any property in the estate of a deceased Native not devised by will should devolve and be administered according to Native law and custom, but this provision was deleted by Act No. 9 of 1929, thus leaving the way open for the promulgation of regulations under the powers granted to the Governor-General by sub-section 10 of section *twenty-three* of the Act. If we examine Government Notice No. 1664 of 1929, we find that it deals with the intestate estates of deceased Natives domiciled outside the Union, holders of letters of exemption in Natal, Natives married in community of property or by ante-nuptial contract and detribalized Natives generally. The object clearly was to deal with these estates in a different manner to those of ordinary tribal Natives. The regulations do not include the estates of those Natives whose only marriage was one out of community of property by virtue merely of sub-section (6) of section *twenty-two* of Act No. 38 of 1927 (which re-enacted in slightly modified form Section 5 (1) of Proclamation No. 142 of 1910). In the opinion of this court, this constitutes a *casus omissus* in cases where there has been no prior customary union, but it is not of any consequence in the present enquiry, where the deceased was first married in community of property. The words used in paragraph (c) of Government Notice No. 1664 are clear and definite and admit of only one meaning, namely, that if the deceased had at any time contracted a marriage in community of property or by ante-nuptial contract his estate on his decease had to devolve as though he had been a European. If this paragraph was intended to apply only to the estate of the parties to that particular marriage, it would have been a simple thing to say so. That this was not done shows that the regulations were meant to apply to a Native who had, as it were, divorced himself from ordinary Native law by availing himself of the special facilities and privileges provided under the ordinary Common law and the number of his marriages and the form thereof did not affect the position.

The question as to what effect this paragraph would have in a case where such a Native, after the dissolution of his Common law marriage, contracted a Native customary union and allotted property to his customary union partner is a thorny one and, fortunately, does not need to be decided in this case. A further complicating factor in Native succession is introduced by Section 19 of Proclamation No. 227 of 1898, which provides that the property of a deceased holder of a quitrent title issued under that proclamation shall, if he dies without a will, devolve according to Native law and custom. This section makes no distinction between Natives married by Christian or civil rites and Section 23 of the Proclamation expressly prohibits the devising by will of the allotment for which he holds title *and of other immovable property.*

These points are mentioned to show the necessity for a comprehensive overhauling of the law relating to Native succession.

This court feels that there is no room for doubt as to the intention of the legislature in framing the regulations under Government Notice No. 1664 of 1929. As the late Daniel Shata had during his lifetime contracted a marriage in community of property, his estate must devolve as though he had been a European and the fact that he contracted a second marriage, which itself did not fall within the terms of paragraph (c), does not affect the position. That being so, it becomes necessary to ascertain whether the appellant (Julia Shata) is entitled to the benefits of Act No. 13 of 1934. In the court below it was argued that this Act was passed to protect Europeans as a class and that it could not override Act No. 38 of 1927, which indicated the intention of the legislature that succession in Native estates should be according to Native custom, and, as the Native estates, would mean practical total exclusion of succession by Native children.

There is nothing in Act No. 13 of 1934 to show that it was passed to protect any particular class, for it speaks of the surviving spouse of "every person", and, consequently, if this Act repealed by implication Act No. 38 of 1927 then, undoubtedly, every Native estate would be affected. It is, however, a well recognized principle in the interpretation of statutes that a subsequent general Act does not affect a prior special Act merely by implication and the maxim *generalia specialibus non derogant* applies. As it was put by the Privy Council in *Barker* v. *Edgar* (1898, A.C., at page 754): "When the legislature has given its attention to a separate subject and made provision for it, the presumption is that a subsequent general enactment is not intended to interfere with the special provision unless it manifests that intention very clearly." In *Garnett* v. *Bradley* (3 Appl. Cases, 944) Lord Hatherley said: "An Act directed towards a special object or special class of objects will not be repealed by a subsequent general Act embracing in its generality those particular objects unless some reference be made, directly or by necessary inference, to the preceding special Act."

The subject of succession to the estates of Natives is fully dealt with in Act No. 38 of 1927, and there is nothing in Act No. 13 of 1934, which, directly or by necessary inference, indicates that the legislature intended in any way to deal with those estates. Accordingly, where the property in a Native estate is in terms of the regulations under Government Notice No. 1664 of 1929 to be administered in accordance with Native law and custom, Act No. 13 of 1934 is inoperative, but where the property has to devolve as if the deceased had been a European, Act No. 13 of 1934 will apply and, in terms of Section 1 (1) (b) thereof, the surviving spouse is entitled to succeed to the extent of a child's share or to so much as does not exceed £600 in value (whichever is the larger).

As the estate in question is admitted to be under £600 in value Julia Shata would appear to be entitled to succeed to the whole estate and is entitled to the interdict claimed.

The appeal is allowed with costs and the judgment in the court below altered to "Interdict confirmed with costs"; the costs of appeal and costs in the court below to come out of the estate.

As the issues in this case were complicated and necessitated exhaustive research into the law of succession, the fee for conducting the appeal is increased to £3 3s.

BIBLIOGRAPHY

Bodenheimer, Edgar. *Jurisprudence*. 1940. New York: McGraw-Hill.

Cardozo, B. N. *The Nature of the Judicial Process*. 1921. New York: Yale University Press.

Cory, Hans and Hartnoll, M. M. *Customary Law of the Haya Tribe, Tanganyika Territory*. 1945. London: Lund, Humphries.

*Diamond, A. S. *Primitive Law*. 1935. London: Longmans, Green.

Fifoot, C. H. S. *English Law and its Background*. 1932. London: Bell.

Lee, R. W. *Introduction to Roman-Dutch Law*. 4th ed. 1946. Oxford University Press.

Lewin, Julius. *Outline of Native Law*. 1944. Johannesburg : R. L. Esson.

Natal Code of Native Law. 1932. Johannesburg : Witwatersrand University Press.

Phillips, Arthur. *Report on Native Tribunals in Kenya*. 1945. Nairobi : Government Printer.

Pittman, William. *Criminal Law in South Africa*. 2nd ed. 1946. Grahamstown: Grocott and Sherry.

Ramsay, T. D. *Tsonga Law in the Transvaal*. 1941. Pretoria: Native Affairs Department.

*Schapera, I. *Handbook of Tswana Law*. 1938. Oxford University Press.

Seagle, William. *The Quest for Law*. 1941. New York: Knopf.

Selected Decisions of the Native Appeal Court (Cape and Orange Free State). 1931— Pretoria: Government Printer.

Selected Decisions of the Native Appeal Court (Transvaal and Natal). 1931— Pretoria: Government Printer.

*Seymour, W. M. *Native Law and Custom*. 1911. Cape Town: Juta.

*Stafford, W. G. *Native Law as practised in Natal*. 1935. Johannesburg: Witwatersrand University Press.

*Whitfield, G. M. B. *South African Native Law*. 1929. Cape Town: Juta.

Wille, George. *Principles of South African Law*. 2nd ed. 1945. Cape Town : Juta.

* Out of print.

ACKNOWLEDGMENTS

The editors of the journals listed below have kindly permitted me to include in this book articles that were first published by them. I have made a few slight changes where they were desirable. The third part of the third essay has not been published hitherto.

1. *Bantu Studies*, Vol. XV. 1941.

2. *Race Relations*, Vol. VII. 1940.

3. *Bantu Studies*, Vol. XV. 1941.

4. *Modern Law Review*, Vol. III. 1939.

5. *South African Law Journal*, Vol. LVIII. 1941.

6. *South African Law Journal*, Vol. LXI. 1944.

7. *Race Relations*, Vol. XII. 1945.

8. *The Howard Journal*, Vol. V. No. 4. 1940.

9. *Africa*, Vol. XIV. 1944.

10. *Journal of Comparative Legislation and International Law*, Vol. XXIV. 1942.

11. *African Studies*, Vol. III. 1944.

12. *African Studies*, Vol. IV. 1945.

The extracts from the reports of the Native Appeal Courts are reproduced by permission of the Government Printer (copyright authority No. 363 of 28 February, 1941).

Pennsylvania Paperbacks